FREE HELP FROM UNCLE SAM TO START YOUR OWN BUSINESS

(OR EXPAND THE ONE YOU HAVE)

THIRD EDITION
COMPLETELY REVISED

William Alarid
Gustav Berle, Ph.D.

Puma Publishing Co.
Santa Maria, California

First Printing May 1988
Second Printing August 1988
Third Printing November 1988
Fourth Printing July 1989 Completely Revised
Fifth Printing October 1989
Sixth Printing June 1990
Seventh Printing August 1991
Eighth Printing February 1992 Completely Revised
Ninth Printing January 1994

Library of Congress Cataloging-in-Publication Data

Alarid, William, 1936–
    Free help from Uncle Sam to start your own business (or expand the
one you have) / William Alarid, Gustav Berle. — 3rd ed., completely rev.
    304 p.   cm.
    Includes bibliographical references and index.
    ISBN 0-940673-54-1 $13.95
    1. Small business—Government policy—United States—Handbooks,
manuals, etc. I. Berle, Gustav, 1920–   . II. Title.
    HD2346.U5A63   1992
    338.6'42'0973—dc20   91-34219
                                                                     CIP

Acknowledgements

Thanks to Terri Nigro, Jay Veneaux, Dan Poynter, and Sam Dawson for their help.

A special thanks to Curt Scott, who, as usual, made an outstanding contribution despite the fact that he was recovering from a near brush with death.

We would like to thank the following people in the U.S. Government for helping us gather this information.

Commodities Futures Trading Commission
  Herb Jackson
Department of Agriculture
  Randall Torgerson
  William Dunton
  Colleen Feist
  Freeman Buxton
  David Salmon
  Mary Lassani
Department of Commerce
  Paul Christy
  James Maruca
  John Kort
  Frank Deliberti
  Gary Young
  Jerome Greenwell
  Walter Bastian
  George Lewett
  Carroll Brickenkamp
  M. Kravanja
  Stephen Gates

  Edward Lehman
  Joann Anderson
  Christiane Simonton
Department of Defense
  Dolores Mahon
Department of Energy
  Effie Young
  Aleta Egeland
Department of Health and Human Services
  Richard Clinkscales
Department of Housing and Urban Development
  Clarence White
Department of Justice
  Enos Roberts
Department of Labor
  Edwin Dean
Department of State
  Laverne Drummond

Department of the Treasury
Debra Sonderman
Shirl Kinney
Department of Transportation
Alicia Casanova
Environmental Protection Agency
Karen Brown
Lynn DePont
Department of Preventive Medicine
Jill Hawkins
Export-Import Bank of the United States
Bert Lomax
Federal Communications Commission
Patti Smith
General Services Administration
Brenda Johnson
Linda Hornsby
Gloria Johnston
Mirinda Jackson
International Trade Commission
Mary Grumble
Interstate Commerce Commission
Dan King
Labor Mediation and Conciliation Services
James Power
NASA
Patricia Mortensen
Overseas Private Investment Corporation
Beth Leach
Eric Luhmann
Securities and Exchange Commission
John Heine
Small Business Administration
Calvin Jenkins
Catherine Funkhouser
Andrew Schneider
J. Glenn Harwood
Andrew Schneider
John Edson

Table of Contents

Chapter 6: Everything You Ever Wanted To Know, But Were Ashamed To Ask (Or, Questions That Would Make Dr. Ruth Blush) 77

Chapter 7: Financial Help 93

Introduction

Every period in our history produces gems of wisdom and often humor. The latter is sometimes quite self-deprecating. For instance: The 1991 recession had one executive stating, "What recession? I sleep like a baby. Every three hours I wake up and cry."

In down times or up times, entrepreneurship goes on and on and on like the Energizer. There always are and always will be those who say "to hell with prognosticators." These men and women see an opportunity, an opening in the economic fabric of our nation, and they jump into it with both feet, or head first. Never mind that only 80 percent of them will survive the first five years.

The true entrepreneur is a bit of a gambler, but a concerned and calculating gambler. The more knowledgeable he is, the greater his or her chances of survival. Knowledge, then, is the ace in the hole. Money? Sure, that's important, too. Money is vital as a lubricant, but it is not the driver who steers the vehicle. The **entrepreneur** is the driver and he or she is first of all motivated by knowledge and all the human characteristics that make up that very complex and somewhat mysterious homo sapiens, the entrepreneur.

Money comes next. And that is the topic we take on in this book. Money is number 2. Much money flows from one of the thousand agencies and offices of the Federal government and that of the 50 states. Not that Uncle Sam's money is a leaky faucet—quite the contrary. Money from Uncle Sam is getting more difficult to tap—but not impossibly so. It just takes know-how and know-who.

Throughout this revised edition of **Free Help from Uncle Sam**, we have trod on the side of fiscal conservatism. The sources we have listed and the suggestions we have made are realistic and pragmatic ones. We have tried to eliminate the blue sky and rose-colored glasses that some books focus on.

Uncle Sam's money, don't forget, is **our** money. The only source of income for the treasury of the United States is your and my taxes. As the custodian of our money, our government is charged with dispensing—investing, if you will—some of that money in viable private businesses. In order to get that money, we in private enterprise must regard the source as realistically and honestly as we do the neighborhood bank.

The government, on the other hand, has become more banker like, since those lush days of free and easy money during the halcyon Johnson years. Now every application for Uncle Sam's money (that is, **our** money!) must be accompanied by commercial bank turn-downs, by financial statements, valid collateral, pragmatic cash flow schedules, and a credible payback plan. There are few exceptions. Normally, you wouldn't want those "exceptions"—disabilities, disasters, dramatic social disadvantages—that could result in direct government loans at lower interest rates. However, in these exigencies, such loans do exist and it is only right that you should know about them.

In this revised edition we have also emphasized more and new case histories and success stories. Few portions of a written record are as inspirational and stimulating as actual life happenings from which we can draw experience and incentives. Also, included are new contacts, updated addresses, and phone numbers that are accurate up to publication time.

More emphasis has also been placed on entrepreneurial areas that are growing—such as international trade (primarily export) and minority enterprises.

We must also recognize some new trends of the Nineties. More and more men and women in their middle years are getting their "parachutes" and are floating to earth without a preconceived place to land. These people are squeezed out by increasing corporate mergers. Many of them are mid- to upper-level executives who, instead of the old golden watch, are sent into temporary "retirement" with a sizable pension fund poke or financial settlement. Members of the Armed Forces and even longtime employees of Civil Service are taking early retirement. In most cases these men and women take with them profound skills and accumulated fiscal security. Many of these will apply these twin assets to new businesses, or to the acquisition of existing businesses. Sometimes these skills and contacts can even be converted into doing business with their former employers.

Approximately 750,000 entrepreneurs will start a business in 1992 and in every subsequent year. Most of them follow their dreams regardless of the risks inherent in entrepreneurship. However, be mindful of the reality that the business person who minimizes the risk is the one who is going to survive—and prosper—the longest and best. Usually, inspiration, enthusiasm, motivation, hard work and persistence are great propellants. Knowledge, nonetheless, is the glue that holds them all together. Money is the great lubricant that keeps them all flowing. Much of that funding comes and flows through the agencies of the U.S. and the state governments.

How to get some of that money, where to get, and from whom to get, is the job of **Free Help from Uncle Sam**. . .

It is up to you now to find the right reference and to follow the rules. Be complete, be realistic, and be professional about your contact and follow-up. Be patient, too. The U.S. Government is a vast bureaucracy, sometimes staffed by brilliant fellow-citizens, sometimes by time wasters who are just waiting for pension-time. Often it seems like all that red tape is not worth the efforts, but remember that it is **your** money that you are applying for—and that the purpose of your request must be to generate profits and benefits for you and yours and for your fellow citizens.

If all else fails and you seem to get swallowed up in red tape or run into a bureaucratic brick wall, pick up the phone from anywhere in the country, and call (800) 827-5722. The answer to your problem might very well lie on the other end of the line.

William Alarid/Gustav Berle, Ph.D.

February 1992

The Authors

WILLIAM ALARID

is an entrepreneur who has used government aid to start several small businesses. He is the author of two business books. Alarid is an engineer, a member of Mensa and is listed in *Who's Who In California*. He lives in Santa Maria, California with his wife, Casey, his daughter, Christine, and his son, David.

GUSTAV BERLE

is a former marketing and communications director of SCORE, the Service Corps of Retired Executives, an affiliate of the SBA and the world's largest volunteer business counseling association. He started and operated several small newspapers and magazines and taught marketing at the University of Baltimore for 18 years. He is the author of nine business books for such publishers as McGraw-Hill, Prentice Hall, John Wiley & Sons, and Puma Publishing. Berle holds a Ph.D. in business administration. He lives in Washington, DC.

Chapter 1

Success Stories
About Some of Uncle Sam's Citizens

With 1,000 different loan programs, two dozen agencies, and Congressionally mandated "ombudsman" departments in every Federal agency—most of them designed to help underprivileged and minorities to get a fair shake—success stories reported by the SBA and its supported agencies (SCORE, SBDC, SBIR, *et al*) dominate the news. Often overlooked, however, are success stories from other agencies such as the Department of Commerce, Department of Agriculture, and Department of Energy. Here are a few from which you might draw helpful inspirations. Taking advantage of them can save you many $$$.

Zero-Cost Consultant Spots Problem

VIENNA, VA—This couple bought a 5 year old going quick-print shop with four employees. Within a year they ran into many problems: primarily, they were unable to do more than break even. Somebody introduced them to a management consultant who charged them $80 for the first session. As the shop owners anticipated a long consulting relationship at considerable costs, a friend told them about the Washington area SCORE office. An experienced management expert from SCORE quickly pointed to the problem: employee inefficiency. It was a tough decision, but one man was laid off and a profit leak in the business was immediately plugged. "Five out of six small businesses fail during the first two years," said the counselor, "due firstly to poor management, and secondly to lack of adequate financing."

Seven Percent Interest Reduction

VALPARAISO, IN—After 22 years as an employee in the food industry, this man decided to go into the wholesale meat packing business with his three sons. They obtained financing through the SBA but at high rates existing at that time—15½%. Within a few months it became clear that the business could not take off as quickly as anticipated, and that the onerous financing terms were making survival impossible. An old friend who was now a counselor with the nearby SCORE office went to bat for the new entrepreneur and arranged with the SBA rescheduled repayment at 8½%. Now, nearly seven years later, the business is prospering and its products can be found from Detroit to Chicago.

Score Team Helps Float Business to Success

BOISE, ID—A vacation in the Idaho River country led San Francisco businessman, D.T., into a partnership with a local river raft builder. From 1986 to 1989 the company's quality products enabled it to grow from $250,000 to $750,000 annual gross. However, such rapid expansion brought its problems—purchasing, scheduling, inventory control, production snafus and managing employees which had grown from three to 11 people. A call to the local SBA office got them in touch with a retired Boise Cascade executive who was now a volunteer SCORE counselor. With his continued help and another experienced volunteer, new production schedules were worked out and quality products restored. The SCORE counselors have become an integral part of the company's team and at no cost to the company. This was truly free help from Uncle Sam!

Cemetery Saved from Going Under

ALBERT LEA, MN—Privately owned and operated cemeteries can be big business, but like all enterprises, they are subject to the risks and frailties of private enterprise. The local burial facility had been a family-owned business since 1973. However, in the past years it had undergone a number of acquisitions by absentee owners. Advance payments for graves and a mausoleum were absconded and the property was embroiled in litigations and bad public relations. While the State files charges against the latest owners, investors in the cemetery banded together and formed a cooperative association, obtained the court's approval to try and save the company, and brought in a SCORE team from nearby Minneapolis to offer a revival plan. More than 500 lot owners were located, brought together, and offered the SCORE reorganization plan. The latter's hands-on assistance and the establishment of a volunteer board of directors brought the nearly defunct cemetery back to life again.

Takes Community by Storm after Tornado

COUNCIL BLUFFS, IA—A July tornado caused $30,000,000 worth of damage and the local mayor called in the local SCORE chapter to get the town back into business. Within six days, 18 members met to map out a rescue plan. One hundred, thirty-four businesses were damaged; $4,500,000 was needed; 105 workers put back to production. SCORE assisted in getting disaster loans and Federal re-training programs, becoming an arm of the small municipal staff and helping 131 businesses to open again.

Incubator Breeds Small Business Success

GOLDEN, CO—The Business and Innovation Center, called an **incubator** because it "hatches" fledgling businesses into full-blown enterprises. It has, on an average, 14 tenants in its

8,500 square feet of space at the Denver West Office Park. An SBDC center is also located here as well as a nearby SCORE office, whose members volunteer their time to help new, small businesses become successful. Partial support comes from private industry through corporate membership. Subsidies usually operate for the first three years of the small businesses accepted into the incubator program. The incubators are expected to grow into self sufficiency within that time and "graduate" into outside facilities. Most incubator facilities are affiliated with universities, where professional and academic personnel are available to assist in guidance and advisory capacities. The National Business Incubation Association is located at One President St., Athens, OH 45701. Phone is (614) 593 4331. The Office of Private Sector Initiatives at the SBA, 409 Third St., SW, Washington, DC 20416 maintains incubator advisory facilities.

Desert Storm Reservists Aided

MINNEAPOLIS, MN—The owner of a local firm was called into service during Operation Desert Storm and was forced to be absent from Spring 1991 to 1992. He was one of several from the area to be dislocated during this military emergency. While wives in some cases took over, the local SCORE chapter jumped into the breech with team assistance on various levels—**at no cost**. The value of such professional services is difficult to estimate, but is indubitably of greater pragmatic value than a bank or SBA loan.

Sweet on Sourdough

SAN LUIS OBISPO, CA—In mid-1983, a couple who loved San Francisco sourdough bread decided that the area was ripe for a hometown bakery that furnished locals with the Golden Bay's famed specialty. They leased a 2500 square foot building, obtained two small loans from a lender who was backed by SBA guaranties, hired one expert employee, lined up two outlets, and began producing 150 one-pound loaves each night. It took but three weeks to increase production, due to word-of-mouth demand. By 1988 the company had expanded into a new 18,000 square foot building and increased its market into much of Southern California. 1991 saw a rise to $3,000,000 in sales, due to the right amount of dough—from San Francisco and the SBA.

Gourmet Cookie Company Kneads Way to Wealth

NEW YORK CITY, NY—The Big Apple appears to be a tough orchard in which to grow a new company. However, a California woman transplanted to New York City opened her own deluxe cookie company after six years of "internship" at a leading hotel. A friend recommended the local SCORE chapter as a counseling resource, and she attended a pre business workshop. One of the counselors helped her in the preparation of a business plan. The latter identified competition, needed production levels for desired cash flow, location and personnel requirements. Her initial "factory" was in a wholesale bakery. She attended local gift shows and utilized trade publications for publicity and small ads. The next year she opened a "test" retail shop and moved into her own baking facility. The assigned SCORE counselor was with her every step of the way and the combined efforts have paid dividends.

International Trade from Deep in The Heart of Texas

MIDLAND, TX—Exporting can originate anywhere in the vast United States. The Texas Department of Commerce passes on leads and inquiries to local SCORE and chamber of commerce chapters. One of them is a local oil and gas drilling operation. In addition to passing on the sales lead from a company in the Philippines, the local SCORE chapter invited the oil company to an international trade seminar. Result: profitable export of equipment produced by existing facilities, all at no cost to the company.

Business Higher Than A Kite

SAN DIEGO, CA—Two brothers who, as boys, loved flying kites, realized their young dreams by going into the manufacturing of scientifically designed kits. Of course, in the growing-up process, one of the brothers became an aeronautical engineer with an MBA from USC, while the other became an engineer-designer. A "big brother" was added when the local SCORE office was approached for some free business assistance to the new company located in a garage. The SCORE counselor, with experience in export, advised them to look into foreign trade. A trip to Japan resulted in a working relationship with the huge Sony Corporation. The business is still a family affair (mother is the number one helper) and is prospering. Says one of the brother partners, "I never thought we'd get in so far, so fast."

Committee Scores 100% Loan Acceptance

SALEM, OR—Getting a loan for a new or small expanding business is often the hardest job, especially when you really need the $$$. In Salem, the local SCORE chapter, headed by a banker, formed a mini-loan committee that guides applicants from the business committee in preparing the proper applications and steers them through the local banks. Of five recently-recommended loan applications, all were accepted by banks. The prime reason: the committee approved workable or realistic budget figures before the applications were turned over to the banks—and evidently the latter agreed.

One-Stop "Business Connection" Helped by SBA

PHOENIX, AZ—The Arizona Business Connection is a one-stop center for small businesses. It was established by the Arizona Department of Commerce and two area SCORE chapters. A statewide toll-free telephone allows easy calling. Local SCORE chapters follow up call-ins with check-up calls and further counseling where this is desired. The SBA's and Arizona's outreach program to small businesses is a great inspiration for other areas and states to follow and enhances the government's free services to the business community.

SBA Deposits $450,000 in Schnitzel Bank

SHEPHERDSTOWN, WV—Running a successful restaurant is the dream of thousands of entrepreneurs. Love does, indeed, go through the stomach. However, restaurants can also become investors' nightmare. The Bavarian Inn, run by restaurant pros from Munich, Germany, Erwin and Carol Asam, is a shining exception of a dream come true. Started in 1977, the inn has grown annually. Ten years ago, local banks put together $750,000 to help the business expand, and the SBA, approached by the banks, added another $450,000 the following year. This infusion of capital enabled the inn to increase its volume from $600,000 to $1,000,000. Now sales are in the $3,000,000 class and nearly a hundred people find employment here. Superior food and accommodations, backed by real expertise and financial security enabled this very tricky business to become an annual award winner.

Hazardous Waste Companies Have Rosy Opportunities

MIAMI, FL—One of the nation's pioneers in hazardous waste management, control and disposal is Enviropact, Inc. They started in 1976, with more foresight than experience. By 1984, they had grown in importance and size, so that the SBA guaranteed a bank loan of $430,000 to expand the operation. The company paid it back in less than four years. Revenue in those days was less than $3,000,000. It has since then skyrocketed to more than $30,000,000, while employees, now over 300, have also increased proportionately. Opportunities in the environment are prolific. EPA, SBA, and virtually every government agency has financial aid programs for the alert entrepreneur in this field.

Hispanic Firm Plays Winning Ball with SBA

MORTON, TX—Ben Ansolabehere (he is of Basque origin) runs a company called Great Western Meat Company. It employs about 300 people, mostly Mexican-Americans, and does around $40,000,000 in annual business. Bank in 1976, when Ben first started, he got a boost from the SBA with a $300,000 loan, supplemented since then with 500,000 dollars. The investment was worth it and loans have been repaid. Great Western now exports $36,000,000 of horse meat to France, sells equine organs to pharmaceutical companies for serum production, and the horse hides to baseball manufacturers. In fact, 40% of America's baseballs are covered with leather produced in Morton, Texas. It has been a win-win game for all sides.

Baby Superstore

GREENVILLE, SC—A score of years ago, Jack Tate graduated from Harvard as a young lawyer. Two years later, while wife, Ginny, was raising their own baby, lawyer Tate changed law books for diapers and opened a large baby store. The very first year, a combination of timing, good research, and hard work, helped the Tates reach a volume of $500,000. Within eight years, expansion of the business, now called Baby Superstore, enabled the SBA to come up with an expansion loan of $460,000. Today the firm has over two dozen franchise stores, annual sales of $27,000,000, and employs over 350 people in their stores, averaging 20,000 square feet each. Success came before the $$$, but the SBA helped to lubricate the company's growth at the right time.

Hot Dog! Maine's Small Business Person of The Year

H. Allen Ryan worked for a hot dog and lunch meat producer in the state of Maine. With the SBA's help he transformed it into a dynamo offering 4,000 different food and non-food items to 1,400 restaurants, schools, and hospitals.

"The local bank insisted on an SBA guarantee as part of their commitment, meaning that without SBA's help the whole deal was likely to die," disclosed Ryan.

"I found SBA to be detailed, professional, and very helpful during the negotiations for the guarantee. They asked tough questions as they sought to balance the interests of the taxpayer and their responsibility to assist small companies. In the end, they saved our deal."

"Without SBA's help I might not own our growing business today."

The Fastest Growing Hispanic Firm in Arizona

And the tenth fastest in the nation is Roberto Ruiz's Maya Construction. With the SBA's help sales went from $1,700 a year in 1978 to $23,000,000 in 1987.

Ruiz has built everything from schools at Fort Huachuca to a water distribution system (including drinking fountains) for the National Park Service in the Grand Canyon. Maya has had private and state building, roadway, and underground water and sewer projects, as well.

Seeing himself "as a coach, not a captain" of his company, Ruiz likes to act "as a cheering section for employees, to tell them when they're on target and guide them when they're not." Twice a year, he retreats with his top managers for two days to plot Maya's business future.

Ruiz has garnered many accolades: Arizona Small Business Person of the Year (1983): National Minority Contractor of the Year, Department of Commerce (1984), and Department of the Interior (1986). SBA likes to think of itself as a cheering section for this intrepid Mexican-American.

Federal Express: SBA Was There at The Creation

Federal Express vice president Fred Smith, whose family founded Dixie Greyhound, started his air package delivery service in May 1973 in Memphis, Tennessee.

Undercapitalized and overreaching, the company had lost close to $7,000,000 by summer. There was no partial bail-out possible—Smith determined he needed no less than $24,500,000 of investment capital (to be matched by banks) in order to service the dozens of cities that would make the new delivery concept both profitable and efficient. Meanwhile, as one report put it, "the company was being held together with bailing wire."

SBA's Small Business Investment Companies (SBICs) supplied 20 percent—or roughly $5,000,000 —of financing needed by Federal Express in 1973 when the young firm was in its critical start-up years.

Some 51,000 people are working at Federal Express (up from only 518 at the time of SBA's involvement). The $3,000,000,000 company created a new concept in hard copy delivery and a whole industry of competitors as well.

From A $75 Parking Lot Striper Machine to Riches

Steven Neighbors of Boise, Idaho swept parking lots as a schoolboy. He noticed that many lots needed fresh stripes to guide drivers into parking spaces. When the opportunity to purchase a $75 striping machine came along, he took it.

"I had a dream to start a road-striping business and was not taken seriously by anyone but the SBA. Their personnel listened seriously to a kid who looked fifteen, and set in motion for him to be trained to consider market, project goals, cash flow, etc. In essence, the Small Business Administration, with the commitment of a direct loan of $10,000 and an investment of time, created a small businessman."

That time investment was provided chiefly by SBA's SCORE counselor Jim Cheatham, a retired engineer, and Nancy Guiles, a loan officer, in the Boise district office. The result is business history. Neighbors' company, Eterna-Line Corp., has been listed among *Inc.* magazine's 500 fastest-growing private companies in each of the past three years. Annual sales went from $5,000 at the time of the SBA loan to $10,000,000 today. Currently there are 200 employees.

Canvas Tarps Made in a Basement

He invented a beltless tarp that rolls automatically over a truck full of grain. His hardwood veneers adorn many a renovated home across the land. But what makes Ed Shorma most happy is that there are at least fifteen nationalities among his 220 employees at Wahpeton Canvas in North Dakota.

You wouldn't expect Malaysians and Indonesians to work in 30-below-zero weather, or what Northerners call "white-out" storms. But Shorma has sponsored dozens of refugees from many lands, and has gone one step further: he has given them jobs.

Up-from-the-bootstraps stories don't involve SBA—that's the conventional misconception. In 1970, after an unsuccessful stint at farming and a term in the state legislature, Shorma wanted to go full tilt with canvas-making. To effect a move from a basement to a downtown space, SBA loaned Shorma $75,000. The extra space was put to immediate use manufacturing original equipment seats for Canadian farm equipment makers—helping the trade balance in the days when it wasn't so unbalanced.

At the time of SBA's first loan, Wahpeton Canvas had gross annual sales of $147,000, and seventeen employees. Today the company sells $12,000,000 worth of goods a year, and has 220 employees. Not a bad return on investment!

The Pickle King

Like relish on your hot dog? Have a yen for sweet (or dill) pickles? Chances are sometime in the past thirty years, most Americans have enjoyed a product of Atkins Pickle Company of Atkins, Arkansas. Think of the Ozarks the next time you taste a good, long, green pickle. And think of

SBA—without it Atkins would have been a pretty puny pickle packer indeed.

In 1959 the pickle company received a $350,000 SBA loan when it had less than $1,000,000 in annual sales and 100 employees. Today Atkins Pickle has $20,000,000 in yearly sales and 400 employees.

Fired Man Builds Uniform Chain

"I was fired into greatness," jokes Harvey Hafetz of his dismissal from a job as a sales representative for a cosmetics distributor in 1971. Of course, that's today—*then* it was a painful experience.

Harvey's wife, Zena, had decided just that year to leave her job as an elementary school teacher and try another challenge. The couple purchased a small uniform shop in Reading, Pennsylvania, as an investment and to give Zena part-time on-the-job training for a new career. But when Harvey lost his job, he joined his wife at the little store. Z & H Uniforms was born.

Today, the company has twenty retail stores, mostly in shopping malls and eleven leased departments catering primarily to health care professionals. A contract sales department furnishes executive-type apparel, hospitality, food service, and industrial-type clothing to industry.

In 1985 Z & H added ten stores after acquiring a Philadelphia-based competitor's stores with the help of a $600,000 SBA-guaranteed loan from Meridian Bank. The firm had 75 employees then: only three years later, it has 170. Annual sales volume has doubled in that time, from $3,500,000 to $7,000,000.

Fishing Boat Success

Ever heard of a start-up fishing boat? It happens.

In 1986 with a loan of $500,000, SBA helped launch the Huntress II and its captain, Richard Goodwin, into the fishing waters off the coast of Rhode Island. According to James Hague, district director in the Providence office, "Our major consideration in approving the SBA portion of this loan was that under-utilized species such as mackerel, hake, herring, and scup, not widely consumed in the United States, would be processed and exported to foreign markets such as Japan, Spain, and other European countries."

The Huntress II fishing operations employ forty, and annual sales in the first year were $2,400,000, substantially exceeding expectations. In the first half of 1987, sales already matched the figures of the entire previous year. Huntress, Inc., recently purchased a second ship for $1,200,000 which will employ up to fifteen new workers.

"The fishing industry in Rhode Island has always been a risky business," said Buddy Violet of Ocean State Business Development Authority (OSBDA). "But these new boats are to fishing what Babe Ruth was to baseball. Phenomenal!" Violet noted that SBA was a crucial partner in the novel project. The State of Rhode Island "could not have gone anywhere else to cinch the deal but SBA," he said.

Government at Apple's Core

In 1977 an SBA-backed Small Business Investment Company (SBIC) provided $504,000 in equity financing to Steven Jobs and Stephen Wozniak, founders of Apple Computer. The company made $42,000 in profit that year. Only fifteen years later, Apple Computer has annual sales of $6,300,000,000 and employs 10,000 people.

Mexican Restaurant Big Hit

Who said SBA won't back a start-up restaurant?

In 1970, Mariano Martinez, Jr. gathered every resource he could to start a restaurant in Dallas' Old Town Shopping Center. He had $5,000 of his own money, and he borrowed $5,000 from his father, $5,000 from a friend, and $51,000 from SBA. By year's end, Martinez had 60 employees and annual sales of $350,000.

Over the next twelve years, Martinez opened a second restaurant in Arlington, Texas, with SBA help ($390,000 loan), and another in Dallas with a $243,000 loan.

Today, employment at the firm has increased to 200, and annual sales exceed $3,000,000. The original loan is paid, while the others remain current.

How About a Joint?

Osteoarthritis, a degenerative joint disease, affects millions, sometimes requiring an implant. The SBA has participated in many of 300,000 total joint procedures in operating rooms in 1986. Here's how.

Orthopedic implants are traditionally manufactured by giant pharmaceutical corporations. But in 1978, SBA took a chance on a small company in Warsaw, Indiana, called Biomet, whose first-year sales was only $17,000. It guaranteed a $500,000 loan to the owners, Dr. Dane Miller, Niles Noblitt, Jerry Ferguson, and Ray Harroff.

Originally its four owners were the only employees. Today, Biomet today has 530 workers, and annual sales of over $55,000,000. The company's phenomenal success—due to technical innovations and rapid delivery of its implants—has made it the 16th fastest growing NASDAQ (National Association of Security Dealers' Automated Quotation System) company in 1987, and the fifth largest manufacturer or orthopedic implant devices in the world.

Plenty of Bread in the U.S.

Samir Saleh had to flee Lebanon in 1976 when civil war broke out. He came to the U.S. and with his uncle's help started a bakery.

Uncle Moussa also "was aware of the resources of SBA," according to Samir. At first there was a pessimistic assessment by SCORE counselor and internationally known baking consultant Frank Dadon. But soon Fred Fried, a retired Westinghouse financial supervisor and SCORE counselor, was giving the Salehs help with business planning and accounting. Along the way two SBA loans gave the Salehs a boost. In 1983, a $100,000 loan covered new machinery and a small debt to a credit union. In 1986, a loan of $178,000 helped the bakery expand to four times its original size.

"For people in our situation, SBA's assistance is the best thing that ever existed," said a grateful Samir, who cannot see returning to war-torn Lebanon: "The way it looks, we're here to stay. The U.S. is our home." As Joe puts it, "only in America could three young immigrant boys with little previous business experience come so far in ten short years."

Score Classes in an Indiana Prison

"Afraid? You bet we were."

Richard Dasse of the Northwest Indiana Chapter of the Service Corps of Retired Executives (SCORE) recalls when he and his SCORE associate began providing management training seminars in a most unusual place—an Indiana prison. "We feared for our safety, and we really wondered if anyone would have the intellectual capacity or be interested."

Now, after three years of providing assistance at the Westville Correctional Center, Dasse acknowledges, "This is not exactly a Sunday School atmosphere," but adds: "We're tremendously impressed. The interest is great, and we've actually encountered some brilliant individuals."

The courses offered at Westville, a medium-security institution located about an hour's drive from Chicago, are similar to those a small business person might find "on the outside"—a pre-business workshop, one on small business management, another on problems peculiar to small business, and another on small business sales.

Intel—A Giant in Byte-Size Chips

It is the eighth largest manufacturer of semiconductors in the world (and one of only three American companies in the top ten). It is responsible for two of the major post-war innovations in microelectronics that have made today's electronic age possible—large scale integrated (LSI) memory and the microprocessor. Its computer chips, software, and minicomputers drive everything from digital gasoline pumps to scanner cash registers in supermarkets.

It is Intel. And when it was a one-year-old baby company in 1969—with 218 employees and $565,874 in sales—it received SBA-backed Small Business Investment Company equity of $299,390. Today Intel has 19,200 employees and annual sales of $1,900,000,000. It has often approached and even surpassed achievements of rivals Motorola and Texas Instruments—two corporate giants when Intel was a start-up small business.

In 1987, 39% of Intel's total revenues came from abroad, making the company one of the top fifty U.S.-based manufacturing exporters. Who ever thought that a well-placed bit of SBA-backed equity twenty years ago would be a key force in helping to right our trade deficit?

Hardware Store in Wyoming

The number one store in the 1,500-store Coast-to-Coast chain of hardware stores rests in the mountain town of Casper, Wyoming. Says owner Ed Bratt, "If it hadn't been for the SBA loan, I doubt we would have even got off the ground."

In 1974, when Ed and Joyce Bratt tried to find funds to start a retail hardware store, they were shut out by banks. But by year's end SBA came to the rescue with a start-up guaranteed loan of $175,000. "On opening day we sold twelve percent of our inventory," Ed relates. No surprise that the loan was paid off in three years. With ten employees then, the Bratts now employ 39; their annual sales volume is $3,000,000.

Ice Cream Success Despite Troubles

Life with the 140-year-old Applegate Farm in Montclair, New Jersey was anything but bright for Betty Vhay. Since purchasing the dairy farm in 1981 with her husband, Vhay has endured more than the usual set of hard knocks. Money was chronically low; neighbors brought a lawsuit against the farm over "loud" machinery that was making ice cream (and making the place a "hangout" for area teenagers); she went through a bitter divorce. It seemed to her at times that the circumstances of the farm's purchase were an ill omen: after losing an unborn child in a car accident, she had taken $100,000 in settlement money to stake her future on Applegate Farm.

With two children to support by herself, Vhay pulled out all stops in the search for money to help the ice cream operation. Bank after bank turned her down as a credit risk.

Then in January 1987, the Money Store Investment Corporation took a chance on Vhay and provided her with an SBA-guaranteed loan of $170,000. For the first time since 1981, she had working capital, was sole owner, and recorded her first profit.

In 1981, Vhay employed 10; today she employs 52, most of whom are teenagers outfitted with their first job as ice cream barflies. Annual sales in 1987 was $700,000, a sizable increase over the $420,000 figure in 1981.

Mel Farr Scores Touchdown in Cars

For every sports star who makes it big, there are many others who lose out when the limelight fades. Bad management skills, drugs, naive investments—these are only a few of the pitfalls. But Mel Farr, former All-American halfback for UCLA and star runner for the Detroit Lions, stutter-stepped away from those things.

Mel Farr Ford, Inc., in Oak Park, Michigan, is one of the largest car dealers in America, ranked 37th of the nation's top 100 U.S. black-owned businesses by *Black Enterprise*. But Farr does not forget a helping hand.

"When SBA granted my loan it was the very key to what I needed at that time," Farr recalls. "Without it, I more than likely would have had to postpone or even forget about my dream of becoming an automobile dealer."

Retail car sales were bleak in the late seventies. Mel Farr Ford, Inc. was born at that time (1978) and in two years the company had sustained severe losses and employees were halved in number, to 45.

But in 1980, SBA made an auto dealer loan of $200,000 to Farr, when sales were $6,000,000. Today there are two more Mel Farr dealerships (Lincoln-Mercury) in Detroit and Aurora, Colorado, and aggregate sales are $52,000,000. There are 140 employees.

Farr out!

Black Ex-MARINE and Jewish Female Consultant Create United Nations Drilling Company

A black man and a Jewish woman—not your usual business team in critical pre-construction testing! It happened in the Bronx.

In a highly specialized field hardly open to minorities and women, Garrett W. Brown, a Vietnam veteran, and Honie Ann Peacock, a consultant in employee relations, drill for "dirt" samples in the chasms of the Big Apple as Python Drilling and Testing.

1980—their first year—was not a good one for construction. There were nights without dinner and weeks when payroll was met on a credit card. Peacock, a single parent, took two outside jobs and worked full time without pay to help get the fledgling company off the ground. Brown, an ex-Marine sergeant who specialized in heavy construction equipment and diesel engines, brought 20 years of experience in the construction industry to the company. He designed and built their first drill rig in his living room.

Peacock wrote the loan proposal and marketing plan that enabled the company to receive a $50,000 direct loan from SBA which bought them their first big drill rig and truck. Today their 16-person crew has been trained completely from within and represents a virtual "United Nations," including Blacks, Filipinos, Hispanics, Irish, and Finns, both male and female.

Though it has been an uphill struggle to gain the confidence of their numerous clients, Brown and Peacock maintain a positive attitude. And why not? From the time of SBA's loan, annual sales have grown from $30,000 to over $1,000,000.

Doughnut-Making Machine Export Success

Li'l Orbits, a Minneapolis manufacturer of a miniature doughnut-making machine and doughnut mix, turned to the Department of Commerce for export assistance. The Department provided publicity with their New Product Information Service (NPIS) along with a description in *Commercial News* magazine, both distributed widely abroad. The products were also exhibited at a Fast Food Exhibition in Paris, France in March of 1988.

"It looks like we're in the export business to stay," reports Li'l Orbits president Ed Anderson. "Results to date are gratifying. Worldwide publicity through this program has resulted in sales of the machine to firms in Japan, Thailand, Germany, and the West Indies.

These efforts resulted in $575,000 in sales. Inquiries from Jamaica, the Philippines, Singapore, Norway, Korea, and Denmark are expected to yield further sales.

Thermal Bags by Ingrid

A 12-employee, Des Plaines, Illinois firm makes insulated bags for catering and food delivery. In five years the firm has gone from zero to approximately $900,000 in sales.

Ingrid exhibited at a trade show attended by foreign firms but their orders were too large for her to fulfill.

She contacted the Commerce Department's International Trade Administration and described her problem. They had her attend an export financing seminar.

"Now we know how to do it," Ingrid says. "We couldn't have done it without the guidance we received from the Commerce Department."

They now export to England, Norway, Australia, Sweden, the Netherlands, Spain, France, Mexico and Panama.

Rebuilt Transmissions and Engines

Tracom, Inc., a small Fort Worth company, rebuilds automotive transmissions and engines. The Department of Commerce consulted with them about the potential for exporting, identified the appropriate foreign firms and helped prepare a sales letter.

Among other sales was one to an Australian distributor for $470,000!

Sales increased from $250,000 a year to $2,500,000 in 1987. Currently they sell to many foreign markets including the United Kingdom, Kuwait, and New Zealand.

Wholesale Computer Supplies

Digital Storage International, a company with six employees, handles magnetic media such as diskettes, tapes and data cartridges in Columbus, Ohio. A slow domestic market compelled them to look elsewhere. The Department of Commerce's Agent Distributor Service (ADS) helped locate overseas representatives. The Cincinnati DOC office also provided export counseling. This help led to expansion into 28 countries.

Department of Energy Helps Software Firm

The Department of Energy funds projects under its Small Business Innovation Research (SBIR) program. It helped Emerson and Stern Associates, a small San Diego firm, develop software for elementary and junior high students using Apple computers. They then negotiated a licensing agreement with a major software publisher for production and distribution.

Department of Health Helps Launch Firm

Data Sciences had two employees and a good idea. They wanted to develop devices to help gather information for pharmaceutical firms from experiments via an implantable transmitter that monitors numerous body functions. They presented the idea to the Department of Health and Human Services, and received financial backing.

As a result of this help, Data Sciences has grown to 12 people and is selling about $20,000 worth of devices per month.

Department of Defense Funds Research

Ultramet, a Pacoima, California firm, had an idea for a coating for rocket engines that won't corrode and is tolerant of high temperatures. The DOD's Small Business Innovation Research program provided funds to develop it. Ultramet is now selling this product to major aerospace companies.

National Science Foundation Helps Company Fight Pollution

Tracer Technologies, located in Newton, Maine, wanted to build an anti-pollution device. Funds from National Science

Foundation through its Small Business Innovation Research program allowed them to do that. They came up with a gadget that can separate chlorinated hydrocarbons so that they can be burned in ordinary furnaces. A service business was launched as a result.

Pizza Analysis

The owner of a pizza shop was having problems with pizza consistency, and productivity. The Commerce Productivity Center sent information on statistical process control, cause and effect diagramming, and other techniques so he could monitor and analyze the process of preparing pizza, and determine the probable causes of the consistency problem. He was also provided information on providing quality service to the customer, measuring productivity, how to study and improve workflow/equipment location.

Japanese housekeeping "Five S" principles were instigated:
1. sort out the clutter
2. set things in order and standardize
3. shine equipment, tools and workplace
4. share information, no searching
5. stick to the rules.

Other principals that were taught are:
—Clutter hides problems
—Everything should have an "address"
—Storage spaces should be self-regulating through visual controls
—Cleaning equipment is a form of inspection
—Make information easily accessible; for example, place operating procedures on machines.

Cultural Help

The American manager of a small west coast electronics firm was having problems managing the engineers of Singapore and American Chinese descent. The Commerce Productivity Center sent information on the work-related values, attitudes and habits of these ethnic groups which are different than those of American workers.

The Effect of Cold on Workers

A northeast construction contractor's job was delayed by legal problems. Outdoor construction was going to have to be done in winter instead of in warmer weather, as had been planned. The owner wanted to know how much productivity would decline because of cold, inclement weather so he could adjust his prices. The Commerce Productivity Center located and sent formulas and information on how construction productivity is affected at different temperatures.

The Effect of Lighting

A floor plan for remodeling some offices at a company had been developed. The plan called for every worker to have a window in his office or by his desk. The boss didn't think this was a good idea. The remodeling planners called to find out if employees with windows in their offices are more productive. The Commerce Productivity Center researched the problem and offered the findings. Workers with windows are happier, but not necessarily more productive. The real issue is proper lighting. Windows and sunlight aren't necessarily appropriate. The best lighting is that which is designed for the particular tasks being performed; proper lighting improves performance. And lighting can be designed for energy efficiency and save money.

The Effect of Nightshift

A contractor was remodeling an office building's interior during the daytime. The remodeling made so much noise that the building's occupants couldn't get any work done. The occupants got a court injunction forcing the contractor to do the remodeling work at night.

When the night work started, the productivity of the contractor's work force dropped dramatically. The contractor

called for help, the Commerce Productivity Center
researched the problem and found the probable cause.

People have an internal biological clock set by routine. Our
bodies tell us when to wake up, when to eat, and when to go
to sleep. When the workers suddenly shifted to night work,
their biological clocks were disrupted. It produced a
jet-lag-type effect.

Studies show that an individual's productivity can decline
until the biological clock adjusts to the new routine. Also,
there was a stress-producing disruption in the workers'
personal routines and schedules.

Saving Money on Wine

A small winery was losing money and needed to cut its costs.
The winery had also been hiring full-time employees for jobs
that took less than full time. The Commerce Productivity
Center provided information on how to study the production
process to identify waste in areas such as transportation,
work in process, machine setup, non-value adding activities,
storage, defects, *et al*, and on developing multi-skilled,
multi-functional workers.

Help Make A Good Impression

The International Operations Group helps small businesses
with their uncertainties concerning foreign clients. For
example:

—The president of a small consulting company heard that a
potential Japanese client was coming to town the next day,
on extremely short notice, and would be available for
meetings. The International Operations Group helped the
company locate information about the company, its products,
and recent company activities, so that the consultant made a
favorable impression and acquired the Japanese firm as a
client.

Ever Been Buried by Your Work?

A rapid transit system contractor was involved in trenching and excavating and asked for help in protecting his workers. A Department of Labor consultant in OSHA was called for a confidential, risk-free evaluation (i.e., the consultant would not issue any citations for violations of state or Federal safety standards). The consultant arrived the day after a heavy rain and found some workers in a twelve-foot deep trench that was not shored nor sloped. He advised immediate evacuation; the supervisor ordered all workers out of the trench. Ten minutes later the sides of the trench gave way. The workers would have been buried. The consultant showed the contractor a six-step plan to resume work safely.

The Government Cures Headaches

A small auto parts custom electroplating shop with four employees had trouble with the workers having headaches. They had recently installed a gas-fired hot-water boiler. An OSHA consultant analyzed the problem: Carbon monoxide from the boiler was coming into the building because there was no vent to bring fresh air to the boiler, and the exhaust fans, instead of helping, were making the problem worse. The employer, with the consultant's help, was able to fix the problem easily.

Meat Packer Gets Solution to Hazard Problem

A meat packer had employees working on a slippery platform 10 feet above a concrete floor. The employees stood on the edge working with power tools on carcasses suspended from a moving conveyor.

The platform was slippery with animal fat. Guard rails could not be used since they would inhibit the conveyor. The employer contacted other meat packers and found that none of them had a solution.

An OSHA consultant gave a free, confidential, no-hassle safety survey. He recommended the employees wear a body belt with a lanyard attached by a sliding ring to an overhead rail. The employees thought they wouldn't like it, but after trying it found it convenient and comfortable, and it did not slow them up.

Census Data Helps Sales

A manufacturer of corrugated boxes contacted the U.S. Census Bureau to help him analyze his sales in the state of Arizona. At the time he was selling primarily to food packaging companies. Using census data he found the market potential was 15 times larger than he was experiencing. Lumber, pottery, and glass industries in Arizona also needed his products and he successfully marketed to these previously unidentified customers.

A manufacturer of products for dairy farms used census data to locate counties with large numbers of dairy farms. By next determining which were the most prosperous, he was able to optimize his marketing efforts.

Government Publication Brings $2,500,000 in Sales

Barrier Industries of Baton Rouge, Louisiana manufactures an insecticidal paint called "Bug-X." They approached the Department of Commerce, who suggested worldwide exposure in the U.S. Government publication *Commercial News USA*. Information on "Bug-X" appeared in the July 1985 issue and resulted in $2,500,000 in sales. The firm has signed six overseas agents and reports another eighteen under negotiation.

Teenage Landscape Entrepreneur

A Pennsylvania teenager applied for and received a Department of Agriculture Youth Project Loan to start a landscaping business. He purchased all of the necessary equipment and operated the business for three years before moving on to bigger things.

Grant for Solar-Powered Outhouse

A Missouri inventor applied for and received a grant to research and construct a solar-energized outhouse. The Above Ground Aerobic and Solar-Assisted Composting Toilet uses solar energy to decompose waste.

Score Helps Two Young Ladies Launch Butcher Shop

An old-fashioned butcher shop in which you can buy ready-cut and portioned meats, but also obtain cut-to-order steaks and roasts, is the unusual business of a pair of young women from Ohio. The father of one has a meat market in another area and he taught his daughter the business. With the help of a knowledgeable SCORE counselor they were able to draft a credible business plan and obtain an SBA-guaranteed loan of $150,000. The money afforded the two entrepreneurs was used to purchase display cases, a walk-in freezer, smokehouse and double oven. With continued help from SCORE counselors, lots of enthusiasm and hard work, the two women recreated a business that had been a vanishing breed—and customers have been coming from near and far because they learned that the shop's products were truly a cut above.

Score Helps Prevent Loss of Lifetime Savings

This is a negative success story and it could apply to any business anywhere. This one comes from San Diego where a man who had been pensioned from a large company had a bundle of cash to invest. He liked the liquor business—quick turnover, constant business, easy-to-handle merchandise. A business broker offered him two stores on the market for $300,000. Fortunately, even though he had his mind pretty well made up to buy them, he followed a friend's advice and contacted the local SCORE office.

A counselor with long years of liquor store experience did his own investigation of the stores—checking inventory, merchandise, traffic flow, competition, service handling, pricing—and then recommended against the acquisition. It was $100,000 overpriced. The locations were weak. The competition from big chains and discount stores was overwhelming. Despite his enthusiasm, the would-be entrepreneur finally realized the SCORE counselor's wisdom and withdrew his offer—possibly saving his lifetime assets before, like alcohol, they could evaporate.

Score Doubles Jewelry Designer's Business

A jewelry designer in Seattle happened to see a story on SCORE in the papers. It stimulated her to seek free counseling and explore her desire to go into a retail business. The counselor guided her first of all in executing a viable business plan, then advised her on seeking and securing a good location.

A seven step plan was developed under which she doubled her business after the first year. The counselor still helps after four years, including proposing a "Men's Night" promotion before Christmas, which turned out to be the year's most productive sales event.

Rags to Riches for Fashion Designer

The mother of two children, divorced, and struggling along on sheer guts and hard work, the young black designer in Massachusetts heard about SCORE and requested an appointment. Fortunately, the assigned counselor evaluated her talent and enthusiasm accurately.

Her unique use of knit fabrics and design, plus the fact that she is an attractive young black woman, combined to make her a "media event." They planned an extensive publicity campaign that attracted a number of local notables and generated considerable press coverage.

A well-executed projection and business plan enabled her to get an SBA-guaranteed loan that allowed for the addition of several sewing machines and more workers. Currently she heads her own design studio, producing fashions under her own label, and has gone national with her line. She was selected as "Woman of the Year" in New England.

Long-term Relationships with SCORE

Supermarkets are admittedly one of the toughest businesses next to running a restaurant. This Indiana family supermarket has had the longest counseling arrangement of any business in the U.S.—and all with the local SCORE counselors. For sixteen years they have been advised by one or several members of the Service Corps of Retired Executives.

Ownership is now in its second generation. Ironically, the family-owned business was encouraged to take over the vacant premises of a former Kroger supermarket that had a good and established location.

SCORE counseled budgeting, financial planning, quality assurance, promotion and the kind of public relations that chain stores could not provide. They helped the family to get into computerization as well as guide them into each step of planned expansions.

Day Care Center Just Kid Stuff to SCORE

Reading in the papers that day care centers are one of the most needed and hottest enterprises, a man-and-wife team of corporate executives saw an opportunity to go into business for themselves. They decided to start an upscale after-school youth-sitting service for latchkey kids in their Connecticut community.

The local SCORE counselors helped them set up a proper business plan and, to conserve limited capital, suggested a direct mail campaign to specific, higher income neighborhoods. Another counselor suggested publicity for the unique venture that was quite successful.

They opened "Kidstop" with seven young customers. Within the year the business had expanded to 64. "The SCORE counselors were a dramatic help to us," said the owners. "We're going to continue using their expertise."

Ornamental Plant Business Blooms Overseas

A large grower of **ornamental plants** in Florida was trying to sell his plants overseas where a potentially uncrowded and lucrative market awaited him. However, he found that it took more plants to fill a traditional container than he could produce, and more expertise and money than he could manage. So he explored the idea with other growers throughout the state. The result was a cooperative association of growers.

They hired a coordinator-promoter familiar with marketing in Holland and Western Europe. In 1985, the first year of the joint effort, the cooperative group sold $2,000,000 worth.

The best was yet to come, however. A SCORE counselor helped reorganize the co-op and initiate a newsletter and promotion material to use at European trade fairs. In 1986 export volume increased six times to $12,000,000. It currently is $18,000,000 and growing.

Inventor Gets Help from The Department of Energy

A Detroit, Michigan inventor developed a system that senses knocking in an automobile engine and controls the spark timing in individual cylinders. The idea was submitted to the Office of Energy-Related Inventions run by the National Institute of Standards and Technology (formerly National Bureau of Standards).

The invention got a favorable review and the government assisted him in bringing it to market. The inventor licensed his system to Ford Motor Company in exchange for royalties.

Chapter 2

Start-Ups on A Shoestring

You might need less money from Uncle Sam—or any other lender—than you think. One thing about borrowing money from either source: you have to figure on paying it back and usually with interest. So, if you can figure out a way of doing with less money (without, of course, jeopardizing your progress and operation), then why not check it out? Here are a number of small companies that made do with the proverbial shoestring:

Famous Companies That Began on A Shoestring

Long before the current decade, when most of the small companies described in this section were started, a long line of internationally famous corporations began—on the proverbial shoestring. Of course, these are the survivors among many who have disappeared from view. Still, they show some common characteristics that hold as true today as they did a century ago: the need for the product or service in the marketplace, a quality product or service, hard work, measured growth, patience and persistence in balanced measure. For instance:

Pittsburgh PA, 1875: **H. J. Heinz** and a brother start putting homegrown pickles into jars. They sell to local grocers whom they have provisioned with fresh produce from their backyard greenhouse. The teenagers' initial investment was 10 cents. When the current family head, a U.S. Senator, was killed in an airplane in 1991, the corporation was valued at $10,000,000,000.

Portland OR, 1963: To make ends meet, an auditor moonlights by importing athletic shoes from Japan and selling them out of his station wagon. Talking about the venture with his ex-college coach, the latter made some important improvements to the sneakers and launched the venture. The initial $1,000 investment to import the shoes has now turned into a $3,000,000,000 business. The entrepreneurs are Philip Knight and Bill Bowerman and their company is **Nike, Inc.**

Chicago IL, 1942: Who is the largest Black publisher in the U.S.? John H. Johnson, founder and owner of Johnson Publishing Co. (***Ebony Magazine***, *et al*). A half a century ago his business was started with $500. How? He took advantage of an existing mailing list of the insurance company for which he worked. He borrowed 20,000 names and mailed a subscription solicitation for a newsletter he planned to publish. As luck would have it, 3,000 replies poured in with checks and the project was launched. The Johnson publishing empire today is worth nearly $250,000,000.

Louisville KY, 1907: Two teenagers were making a few dollars each week delivering packages for local merchants. By 1915 they had to think seriously about going into business. Model-Ts had become popular and with a $100 down payment, they bought their first delivery vehicle. Today, a couple of generations later, James Casey's and Claude Ryan's little business has thousands of deep brown trucks all over the country with the name United Parcel Service (UPS) stenciled on each side. The worth of the business? About $6,000,000,000.

New York, 1935: It is the depth of the Depression. Josephine Esther Mentzer helped the family by selling a skin-care ointment that her uncle was marketing. Then she got an idea. Rather than selling door-to-door the slow way or to a few local drug stores with little turnover, why not try the high-volume department stores? However, before trying the new outlets, she developed her own line of cosmetics with about $100 in savings. Today these cosmetics are known as Estée Lauder and the company is worth about $1,000,000,000, making the erstwhile Ms. Mentzer one of the world's richest women.

Recent Companies That Began on a Shoestring

Men's Shorts Produce Long Profits

SAN FRANCISCO, CA—Joe Boxer Inc., manufacturer of men's boxer shorts and ties, was established by 24-year-old Nicholas Graham with about $100 in capital. Calling on men's clothing stores and men's buyers at local department stores, he sold them unusually patterned ties made by himself in his bedroom. One buyer suggested using the unusual fabrics to make boxer shorts, and a new line was born. The first year, Graham would up with $600,000 gross volume, and financed his growing operation with factoring all orders at 80% of invoices on the day an order was shipped. All sewing was eventually subcontracted. Now contracting has been farmed out to a plant in China. After 18 months in business, Joe Boxer Inc. reported volume at the rate of $1,000,000 annually. Today, eight years later (1991), the company has 46 employees and grosses $22,000,000 annually.

Real Estate Billing Starts Newsletter

HOUSTON, TX—A part-time real estate salesman in college, Marc Ostrofsky, was inspired to go into the newsletter business. Using the technique he learned in real estate, he collected the first month's payment and the last month's payment of the yearly advertising contract—and with this up front money was able to parlay his new business into two magazines seven years later, grossing $3,700,000 and employing 30 full- and part-time people.

$30,000,000 Business Forms Firm Started Informally

CLEVELAND, OH—A young, trained accountant, Greg Muzzilo was only 23 when he decided that being in business for himself is the only way to go. Business forms, he reasoned, were used by everybody, though he did not realize that it is a highly competitive business. The first few hundred dollars of his own money went into telephone answering machines and a good letterhead. He then opened a line of credit with 25 different business form manufacturers, but vendors were impressed with the youthful enthusiasm and earnestness. He also developed a tough phone technique, masquerading as an implied mob collector, that he used on recalcitrant customers. Thirteen years later, the company does $30,000,000 annually and employs 65 men and women.

UPS Payments Financed Cheeky Start-Up

MEQUON, WI—When you have great ideas for software packages but are only 21 and have but a few hundred dollars in the bank, ingenuity must become a partner. Dan Armbrust did this back in 1983. He bought some floppy discs and put his ingenious programs on the blank diskettes, shrink-wrapped them on a household gadget, and started making cold calls to computer stores. What he sold he collected COD, turning a disk bought for pennies into a retail item sold for as much as $199. He arranged to buy supplies from out-of-state vendors. They then shipped via UPS. Armbrust paid the drivers, but knew he had several days to make good on the checks. Several days' delay was enough to copy the software onto the blank disks, deliver them, and make good on the payments. It was risky, but it worked. Today, eight years later, the company does $16,000,000 in annual revenue and keeps 34 employees on the payroll.

Vietnam Vet Discovers Novelty Business

SAN LEANDRO, CA—Living in the back of a warehouse and eking out a meager living by driving a truck and going to school under the G.I. Bill, Fred DaMert tinkered with polymers. His experiments, designed for family Christmas gifts, turned up a real surprise. His soft prisms reflected natural light in wondrous ways and sparked the idea that he had indeed latched on to a salable gift item. A local chain store buyer ordered 24. Others followed. Then he found that museum stores across the country loved his items. For 18 years now, DaMert has been making a good living, as have his 15 employees and annual business is brisk at about $4,500,000.

Gimmick Business Grows on Brains, Not Bucks

LOS ANGELES, CA—Marc Sirkin, a 25-year-old production manager for a TV show, figured that tinsel town needed somebody with his fertile brain to come up with promotional gimmicks. So, in 1984, with a few bucks, a spare bedroom, and a few friends, he started making T-shirts, jackets, balloons, and plastic replicas to hype various movies. After two years of struggles, he obtained an order for 15,000 emblazoned jackets at $22 each, a $180,000 order, that enabled the mini company to finance itself into major growth. Ingenuity and quick turnaround of orders sparked the growth, not heavy financing. Today the company provides a living for 15 employees and grosses $3,600,000 a year.

Parlaying Pennies in Disney's Shadow

ORLANDO, FL—In the shadow of the Walt Disney empire south of Orlando, Florida, a tourists' newspaper carrying a respectable 64 pages into 200,000 hands is making money for the Kenneys. It was not always thus. In 1982, Dick Kenney, working part-time to support his new idea, started the first of the local tourist newspapers, financed with that month's rent check of $185. The copy was done on an old typewriter. A printer accepted the job on spec. Distribution was done store-to-store by the Kenneys. Enough advertisers paid half of their ad costs up front. A decade later the guides take in $1,000,000 and keep 16 employees busy part- and full-time.

Visors Give Sunny Start to Student Entrepreneurs

ATLANTA, GA—Two college dropouts, restless to get away from theory and into money-producing business, figured that a good sun visor would sell well in sunny Florida. In 1982, they pooled their meager funds and drove down into the Sunshine State. Some weeks of market research later, they came up with a plastic visor that clamped around foreheads without straps or elastics. A local mold maker agreed it was a good item and staked the boys to a free mold in return for two cent royalty on each of an estimated 1,000,000 visors sold. They called their company Alpha Products and turned a fledgling idea into a $20,000,000 success—generating all sorts of other products along the way to success. How did they finance themselves in the early stages? By moving furniture for local stores.

Chapter 3

Assistance and Information

Starters

Where to Go First

Where do you start if (1) you currently are not in business and (2) would like to learn how to avoid common pitfalls and (3) want to take advantage of the experience of others?

The following four organizations will help point you in the right direction:

The Business Assistance Program, formerly known as **The Roadmap Program**, guides business to appropriate contacts. It is run by the Business Liaison Office of the Department of Commerce. They can answer such questions as:

- What sources can help me start a business?

- How can I sell my products or services to the Federal Government?

- Where do I find overseas buyers?

- Where can I get Federal business loans?

- Where can I get information on what the government is buying?

- Where can I find the manufacturer of a particular product?

- What associations serve my industry?

- Where can I get information on patents, trademarks, and copyrights?

- How can I market my invention?

- Where can I get information on exporting and importing?

- Who can advise me on unfair trade practices?

- Where can I get debt collection guidelines?

- Where can I get Federal statistics?

- Where can I get company lists?

- How do I register my company name?

The office develops and promotes a cooperative working relationship and ensures effective communication between the Department of Commerce and the business community. It provides assistance to businesses which desire help in dealing with the Federal Government.

Professional staff members provide guidance through the Federal maze: answer inquiries concerning Government policies, programs, and services, and provide information on published materials on a variety of topics. It also serves as a focal point for Department of Commerce agencies' contact with the business community. Write or call: Nancy Larken, Business Assistance Office, Department of Commerce, Room 5721C, 14th & Constitution Avenue, N.W., Washington, DC 20230. Contact (202) 482-3176.

Federal Information Centers can also help you find the right answer. Often they will have copies of commonly-used forms, such as copyright forms, that they will send from a telephoned request. These centers are a focal point for information about the Federal Government.

Centers assist people who have questions about Federal services, programs, and regulations, but do not know where to turn for an answer. FIC information specialists either answer an inquirer's questions directly, or perform the necessary research to locate and refer the inquirer to the expert best able to help.

There are currently 72 cities with an FIC and an additional 51 cities are connected to the nearest center by telephone tieline. Statewide toll-free '800' service is available to the residents of four states: Iowa, Kansas, Missouri, and Nebraska. For a list of FIC numbers see Appendix 1.

The toll-free Small Business Answer Desk handles about 150,000 inquiries per year. They will send a free "Small Business Startup Kit." You may request this from your local SBA office also.

Run by the Small Business Administration, the Answer Desk is a nationwide, toll-free (800) telephone service to help small business persons needing help or guidance with problems connected with their firm or to deal with the complexities of government. It is an information and referral service guiding callers to the correct source for a definitive answer to inquiries relating to government regulations, government, and private source business assistance.

In most cases, the information or referral requested can be handled immediately by the Answer Desk staff, supported by rotators from all of the SBA's program areas and a variety of resource materials.

The Answer Desk focuses on Federal Government programs and regulations, but also provides information about state, municipal, and private sector agencies. It does not provide legal, accounting, or managerial advice. They refer such inquiries to appropriate sources, such as lawyers, accountants, SBA field offices, and appropriate government agencies.

The Answer Desk enables the SBA to become aware of the problems and issues of the small business community, which ultimately helps government do a better job of helping small business. Call toll-free (800) 872-5722 or, if in the Washington area, (202) 653-7561.

New Business Incubation Centers Referral Service. Information is provided about the location of specific incubation centers which could help a smaller business.

Incubation centers are special facilities which offer a new business the facilities and business assistance which could make the difference in a firm's success. Since most of these centers are new, this office is maintaining a special file of the services and specialization of each center.

Call (202) 653-7880 and ask for Tom Lorentzen or John Shrewder, or write Private Sector Initiatives Office, Small Business Administration, 409 3rd Street SW, Room 317, Washington, DC 20416.

The Best Problem Solvers

Once you've gathered some basic information or start running into problems, try these fixer-uppers:

Services Corps of Retired Executives (SCORE) assists with free business counseling and training. They can get you out of the red faster than Rambo. SCORE exists solely for the benefit of the small business community. For anyone who is in—or is considering entering into—a small business, SCORE offers many services that might well be of critical importance to his or her success. SCORE makes no charge for counseling services, but usually charges a nominal fee for participating in training and workshop sessions.

Small business clients should be encouraged to take advantage of any of the following SCORE services that may meet their needs:

- **Counseling**: Both those who are considering entering a business enterprise and those who are already in a small business may benefit from the experience of successful, retired executives who are familiar with similar businesses. The advice furnished by SCORE counselors may be directed towards solving a particular problem or toward planning for future growth.

- **Training**: Broadly focused pre-startup business workshops are offered periodically, as well as more specialized classes, seminars, and conferences concerning topics of great value to certain segments of the business community. Subjects such as business organization, site selection, trade promotion, marketing, accounting, taxation, and financing are a few examples of the specialized training available.

- **Information**: Advice on obtaining and utilizing the professional services of lawyers, accountants, bankers, advertising agencies, and others, as well as the resources of government agencies, is provided upon request.

The primary purpose of SCORE is to render a community service by providing, without charge, the expert assistance of its volunteer counselors in solving the problems encountered by small businesses. In addition to a substantial number of retired executives and managers, the membership of SCORE chapters throughout the country includes many individuals who have not yet retired from active employment and are enrolled in its ACE (Active Corps of Executives) component. Volunteer counselors who are qualified to furnish specialized counseling and training based upon their extensive and

widely-varied business and professional experience are
selected.

To locate a SCORE chapter near you, look in the blue section
of the phone book for the nearest SBA office or call (800)
827-5722. After the call is answered press "1" on your
touch-tone phone, then press "3" for more information, then
press "1" and enter your area code. You will receive a
recorded list of SCORE phone numbers in your area.
Written inquiries should be addressed to: National SCORE
Office, Small Business Administration, Suite 500, 409 3rd
Street, Washington, DC 20416.

Chapter 4

New Products

E ach year government laboratories invent hundreds of new items which can be licensed by you, often on an exclusive basis. For example, 27% of NASA's patents are turned over to private industry via these agreements. Currently there are over 7,000 patents that are available for license.

License A Government Invention

A weekly newsletter, *Government Inventions for Licensing*, presents summaries (abstracts) of new inventions. All inventions are available for licensing (often exclusive). The newsletter describes some 1,200 new inventions each year. Annually, all inventions are presented in the *Catalog of Government Inventions Available for Licensing*. This catalog arranges descriptions of these 1,200 inventions under 41 subject areas for easy reference.

There is also a service named *Tech Notes*. *Tech Notes* provide illustrated monthly fact sheets of new processes and products developed by Federal agencies and their contractors. Each fact sheet details a specific invention, process, software, material, instrument or technique selected for its potential for commercial development or practical application.

Annual collections of all *Tech Notes* are available as the *Federal Technical Catalog*.

For more information contact: National Technical Information Service (NTIS), Center for the Utilization of Federal Technology (CUFT), Department of Commerce, 5285 Port Royal Road, Springfield, VA 22161. Phone (703) 487-4732.

Getting Your Invention Evaluated (And Perhaps Some Cash Too).

If your invention is energy related, you can get a free evaluation of its commercial feasibility and perhaps a grant to develop it further.

The **Energy Related Inventions Program** encourages innovation in non-nuclear energy technology by helping individual inventors and small R&D companies develop promising energy-related inventions. It evaluates all submitted inventions and recommends those that are promising to the Department of Energy (DOE).

The evaluation criteria are: technical feasibility, degree of energy impact, commercial potential, and intrinsic technical merit. DOE then reviews the recommended inventions and, working closely with the inventor, determines the next reasonable step for the invention and how much money it will take. Most often, support takes the form of a one-time-only cash grant and technical assistance in developing linkages with the private sector.

Contact: Energy Related Inventions Office, National Institute of Standards and Technology (formerly National Bureau of Standards), Department of Commerce, Building 411, Room A-115, Gaithersburg, MD 20899. Phone (301) 975-5500.

Automatic Awareness of What's Being Patented Concerning Your Specialty

If you have a particular interest, it's a good idea to keep abreast of what others are doing. Often after receiving a patent you may wish to contact the inventors or you might get fresh ideas on improving your product without infringement.

Using the **Patent Subscription Service** and establishing a deposit account with the Patent and Trademark Office, businesses can be sent full copies of all appropriate patents as they are issued. Selection is made using any of the more than 112,000 subclasses.

Contact: Patent and Trademark Office, Department of Commerce, Attn: CBIS Federal Inc., P.O. Box 9, Washington, DC 20231. Phone Wan Wu at (202) 377-2535.

How To File for a Patent

The **Patent and Trademark Office** examines patent applications and grants protection for qualified inventions. It also collects, assembles, and disseminates the technological information disclosed on patent grants.

Printed copies of individual patents may be purchased directly from PTO. Printed collections of all new patents are issued each week in the Official Gazette which is available by subscription from the Government Printing Office.

A booklet, *General Information Concerning Patents*, is available from the Superintendent of Documents, Washington, DC 20202 for $2. An information booklet, *Basic Facts About Patents*, is available from the Patent Office.

Contact: Public Affairs Office, Patent and Trademark Office, Department of Commerce, Washington, DC 20231. Phone (703) 557-5168 or (703) 557-3341.

Registering a Trademark

Businesses interested in registering a trademark may contact this office for the information and forms required. An information booklet, *Basic Facts About Trademarks*, is available.

Applications for trademark registration must be filed in the name of the owner of the mark. The owner may file his own application for registration, or he may be represented by an attorney. Trademark applications may be filed before a trademark has been used. However, protection is reduced from 20 to 10 years. It may be re-registered after that period.

Contact: Trademark Information, Patent and Trade-mark Office, Department of Commerce, Washington, DC 20231. Phone (703) 557-4636 or (703) 308-9000.

Obtaining a Copyright

A series of pamphlets and forms is available to assist firms in understanding, searching, or applying for a copyright. Although the office cannot give legal advice, it can assist in providing information on claiming a copyright, what can be copyrighted, notice of copyright, transfer of a copyright, and searching records of the Copyright Office.

Contact: Copyright Office, Library of Congress, Washington, DC 20559. Phone (202) 479-0700.

Where To Get Information on Foreign Research

Technology-oriented businesses interested in staying up to date with foreign government technology will find the efforts of the **Foreign Technology Program** of special value. NTIS maintains formal agreements with more than 90 foreign sources of technical reports. In addition, NTIS receives foreign technical reports collected by other U.S. Government agencies. In all, some 20,000 foreign reports are annually added to the NTIS report collection.

A Bi-weekly newsletter provides useful information gathered from embassy and other sources around the world. Included in the newsletter are abstracts to the current foreign R&D results.

The countries covered by this program include Austria, Australia, Belgium, Canada, Denmark, Finland, France, Germany, Israel, Japan, the Netherlands, New Zealand, Norway, South Africa, Sweden, Switzerland, and the United Kingdom. Most of the reports from these countries are available in English.

Contact: Foreign Technology Program, National Technical Information Service (NTIS), Department of Commerce, 5285 Port Royal Road, Room 306F, Springfield, VA 22161. Phone (703) 487-4820.

How to Develop and Bring a New Product to Market

The Departments of Energy and Commerce, the National Society of Professional Engineers, the National Congress of Inventor Organizations, the Licensing Executives Society, and the American Intellectual Property Law Association sponsor two-day seminars throughout the U.S.

The topics covered are; patenting and protection, estimating the worth of an invention, licensing, marketing, new business start-up, the business plan, research and development, venture financing, and the Department of Energy's Inventions Program and Small Business Innovative Research Programs.

If the new product is energy related, the Department of Energy may provide assistance in developing, financing, and marketing the product.

The seminar applies to all products, whether or not they're energy related.

To get more information, contact: Office of Energy-Related Inventions, National Institute of Standards and Technology (formerly National Bureau of Standards), Building 411,

Room A115, Gaithersburg, MD 20899. Phone (301) 975-5500.

Help to Stimulate the Innovative Process

The **Small Business Technology Liaison Division** and the Industrial Technology Partnership Division work with smaller firms to assist them to better understand the components of the innovative process. They focus on a company's understanding of business tools such as sensitivity analysis, technology screening, and networking resources. They can connect you with other groups involved in innovation.

Training is also provided in R&D (innovation) financing mechanisms and in the innovation process. Training, for individuals and small groups, is customized to requester's needs. It covers: innovation policy; cooperative and joint R&D arrangements; R&D limited partnerships; corporate partnering; Federal and National R&D funding; sources of cooperation between universities and industry; venture capital, and innovation facilitators. A series of special publications is available.

Contact: Office of Technology Commercialization, Department of Commerce, Room 4418, 14th & Constitution Avenue, NW, Washington, DC 20230. Phone Lansing R. Felker at (202) 377-5913.

Stuff Made Out of Wood

It may surprise you to find that the Forest Service serves the private sector with its research to improve the use of wood and to develop wood products.

Its **Forest Product Laboratory** (FPL) in Madison, Wisconsin has developed wood structures such as the **Truss-Framed System**, an innovative way to build homes and light commercial buildings. The system uses 30% less structural framing than conventional construction, can be put up faster by fewer people, and is more disaster resistant.

Builders could realize a savings in construction costs. It has been used in 31 states so far and its use is spreading. The system has been assigned a public patent and can be used by anyone.

A recent product concept is a **lightweight structural fiber panel** called FPL Spaceboard, which is molded from wood fibers. It can be made thinner, lighter and stronger than existing fiber boards. It may have uses in wall, floor and roof panels, in packaging, and in some furniture applications. The spaceboard concept offers a way to use virgin or recycled wood fiber.

The Forest Products Laboratory has publications to meet needs of many users. There are publications lists of interest to furniture manufacturers. architects, engineers, builders and lumber retailers. Other lists cover: packaging (boxes, crates, pallets), adhesives, wood energy (including research on liquid fuels), finishing wood exteriors, fire performance of wood, and wood drying. Materials are also available on subjects such as improvement of sawmill efficiency and recycling of paper and wood wastes.

For more information, write or call Colleen Feist, Public Affairs Specialist, Forest Products Laboratory, One Gifford Pinchot Drive, Madison, WI, 53705-2398. Telephone (608) 231-9240.

Factory of the Future

The Center for Manufacturing Engineering operates the **Automated Manufacturing Research Facility** (AMRF). The main purposes are to address two basic problems in computer-integrated manufacturing:

● provide assurance that small firms will be able to obtain equipment from different manufacturers at different times and have them all work together without expensive custom-designed interfaces.

- find means of controlling quality in a fully automated factory by innovative measurement processes.

Dozens of companies, large and small, have sent their researchers to work in this facility beside their government counterparts. The results have been voluntary standards that are solving the compatibility problem.

In addition, over 36 patents, products, and systems have found their way into commercial use as a result of work at the AMRF.

All machines and computer systems used in the AMRF are made in the U.S. It is expected that 100,000 machine shops, mostly small, will take advantage of this automation technology.

As we are all aware, the U.S. has suffered on quality of manufacture products in the last two decades. AMRF techniques are revolutionizing the manufacturing process to make sure parts are made right the first time and every time. All this is accomplished with less waste, faster, with a set-up time of nearly zero.

Tours may be arranged through this exemplary facility in Gaithersburg, Maryland. Contact: Center for Manufacturing Engineering, Automated Manufacturing Research Facility, National Institute of Standards and Technology, Gaithersburg, MD 20899. Phone Adrian Moll at (301) 975-6504.

Shop of the '90s

Small machine shops fabricate 75 percent of all U.S. metal products. However, they are behind countries such as Japan, Sweden, and Germany in use of modern technology.

Uncle Sam has set up a program to help solve automation problems. Questions such as:

- What modern technologies are commercially available, affordable, and useful to small job shops?

● What return on investment might be expected?

● Where can shop personnel get training?

The **Fabrication Technology Division** of the National Institute of Standards and Technology (NIST) have created a shop similar to a small, privately-owned operation. Only affordable off-the-shelf systems and software are used. Purchases and changes are justified by a reasonable return on investment.

The program reviews and evaluates existing machine tools and resources, uses personal computers for cost estimates, planning, computer aided design and manufacturing, and trains shop personnel in the use of this system.

In 1992 at Albertville, France, the U.S. Olympic Ski Team will use aerodynamic helmets manufactured by small shops from a diskette provided by NIST. The helmet has less drag, is twice as light, and four times stronger than the team's previous helmet.

A **"Shop of the '90s"** seminar center with hardware and software has been established. The center is available to private industry.

For more information contact: Denver Lovett, Mechanical Engineer, Fabrication Technology Division, Manufacturing Engineering Laboratory, National Institute of Standards and Technology, Building 304, Room 136, Gaithersburg, MD 20898. Telephone (301) 975-3503.

Chapter 5

Selling To The Feds
(Or, How To Get Your Tax Money Back)

U ncle Sam can be your best customer; there is no product or service that he doesn't purchase someplace. One of the following should help:

Business Service Centers

Business Service Centers (BSCs) provide advice and counsel to those wishing to contract with the General Services Agency (GSA) or other agencies. GSA Business Service Centers (BSCs) have been established to provide advice and counsel to business persons who are interested in contracting with GSA and other Federal agencies and departments. There are 13 centers nationwide, most of them located in GSA regional headquarters cities. Knowledgeable business counselors, trained to answer all but the most technical questions, are available. Often, BSC personnel are the first direct contact a business representative has with the Federal Government.

BSCs exist primarily to serve entrepreneurs in their search for Government contracts. BSC counselors provide individuals and firms with detailed information about all types of Government contracting opportunities. Copies of bid abstracts, which indicate names of successful bidders, other bidders, and price bids, are available in the centers. Information regarding the total dollar-volume of GSA store stock items and quantity of items sold is also available.

These centers are responsible for issuing bidders' mailing list applications, furnishing invitations for bids and specifications to prospective bidders, maintaining a current display of bidding opportunities, safeguarding bids, providing bid-opening facilities, and furnishing free copies of publications designed to assist business representatives in doing business with the Federal Government.

BCSs also play an important role in the GSA's small business set-aside program and the small and disadvantaged business subcontracting programs. Check Appendix 7 to locate your nearest BSC or call (202) 708-5804.

Selling Cups and Socks and Antique Clocks

If you have a common-use item for sale, while at the BSC ask for the **Public Liaison** staff.

The staff works with suppliers of common-use items and nonpersonal services for Federal agencies. Examples of items include: office supplies and equipment, furniture, tools, hardware, refrigerators, air-conditioners, water coolers, scientific and laboratory equipment, medical, photographic, and audio-video recording equipment and supplies. The various programs under which procurements are made are described in the following sections;

- **Stock Program**: Under this program, a wide variety of common-use items are stored in supply facilities located nationwide for timely and cost-effective distribution to customer agencies.

- **Federal Supply Schedules**: This program provides Federal agencies with sources for products and services such as furniture, electric lamps, appliances, photographic, duplicating, athletic, laboratory, and audio and video recording equipment and supplies. Schedules are indefinite quantity contracts entered into with commercial firms to provide supplies and services at stated prices for given periods of time. They permit agencies to place orders directly with suppliers. Federal supply schedules are published to provide ordering data for these contracts.

- **Special Order Program**: Items sometimes are not suitable for inclusion in either the stock or Federal supply schedule programs. Agency requirements for such items are consolidated by GSA and special definite quantity contracts are executed. Direct delivery is made from the contractor to the agency involved. Information is available on supplying items for these programs and placement on a bidders mail list.

PASS: How To Get Easy Exposure for Your Products and Capabilities To All Government Agencies

You fill out just one simple form that takes about five minutes to complete. At your SBA office (this form is available at many other offices also) ask for **PASS (Procurement Automated Source System)** information. This automated system substantially improves government contract and subcontract opportunities for small businesses.

Through PASS, a company becomes part of a nationwide government agency resource list utilized by headquarter and field procurement offices in the matching of many procurement requirements against capabilities in the PASS database. Major Federal prime contractors also use PASS to identify subcontracting opportunities. The system is based upon the use of selected key words, SIC/PSC codes, geographical locations, and types of firms.

Contact: Your local SBA office or, call (800) 827-5722. Press "1" on your touch-tone phone, then press "7".

Procurement Data

Contact the **Federal Procurement Data Center** in Washington to get procurement information customized for your needs. The center is a unique source of consolidated information about Federal purchases; its information can assist businesses in their planning and marketing efforts. A master database contains detailed information on the purchases by more than sixty agencies. Companies can learn how much the Government spent in each fiscal quarter on items such as clothing, food, furniture, fuel, building materials, ADP services, and weapons.

Two types of reports are available. A free standard report contains statistical procurement information in snapshot form. It also compares procurement activities by state, major product and service codes, degree of competition, and contractors.

Special reports tailored to a specific need are also available. They can be based upon up to 25 data elements which can be cross-tabulated in hundreds of ways. Such a report can help analyze Government procurement data and trends, identify competitors, and locate Federal markets for individual products or services.

Information can include name of Federal agency purchasing offices, product or service and date an agreement was reached, contractor's name and address, dollar amount obligated, extent of competition, and type of business that received an award.

Examples of previously requested topics include:

● who purchased and sold traffic signal systems

- contracts awarded to specific companies for IBM compatibles

- awards to a specific corporation

- construction contracting by state

- contract awards for specific counties or states

- the top 300 contractors of DOD for R & D contracts

- the top 200 product codes ranked by dollars awarded.

On a reimbursable basis, the Center will also provide computer tapes of the entire contents of its database; mailing lists of contractors who sell to the Government sorted by region, product, and service code, etc. and mailing lists of Government purchasing offices.

Call or write: General Services Administration, Federal Procurement Center, Room 5652, 7th and D Streets SW, Washington, DC 20407. Phone (202) 401-1529.

Who Wants What Computer

Contact the **Federal Equipment Data Center** if your specialty is computer-related. The center maintains a Government-wide inventory of all owned and leased general purpose data processing equipment, provided these system components exceed a purchase value of $50,000 or a monthly rental value of $1,667.

Information collected includes the make, model, and manufacturer of each component; the acquisition cost; the agency using the equipment, and the projected date of replacement or upgrade. This information is received from more than 60 Federal departments and agencies, and forms the database for the Automatic Data Processing Equipment/ Data System (ADPE/DS).

This unique data system provides a consolidated source of information about Federal ADP equipment inventory. The available data can be used to analyze where and when large ADP replacement or upgrade may occur, what types of equipment will be involved, where compatible installations are located, and the location of leased equipment. This information can be a powerful marketing tool. The information is accessible through two types of reports.

The ADPE/DS standard report is issued semi-annually and contains statistics and graphics pertaining to manufacturer's market share, age of the inventory, agency inventories, dollar share, and component mix. Special reports, tailored to an individual's data needs, also are available for a nominal charge.

The special reports are available on a reimbursable basis. They can be tailored to a specific need and can be formatted in any way the requestor desires. Information such as the make, model, and manufacturer of the equipment, the city and state where the equipment is located, the equipment's age, whether it is leased or owned, and the planned upgrade dates can be sorted and analyzed.

Call or write: General Services Administration, Federal Equipment Data Center, Room 5652, 7th and D Streets SW, Washington, DC, 20407. Phone (202) 401-1529.

DOD Potential Contractors

If you want to try defense projects, join the **Potential Contractor Program**. The program was established to certify and register non-government organizations for access to Department of Defense scientific and technical information. This includes information on needs, requirements, work, and accomplishments associated with research, development, test, and evaluation. Through this program, organizations are provided the opportunity and means to obtain current scientific and technical information required to maintain their capabilities as developers and producers of military equipment and materials.

Firms, individuals, or activities with a demonstrable capability of performing research/development with a reasonable potential for eventually receiving a contract with DOD are invited to participate in the program.

Contact: U.S. Army Headquarters, phone (703) 274-8948, fax (703) 274-3263. U.S. Navy Acquisition, phone (703) 602-9057 or 602-9058, fax (703) 602-9054. U.S. Air Force, AFIFIO, phone (513) 255-5766, fax (513) 255-5383.

Become Certified as "Competent" Through The *Certificate of Competency Program*

The program will certify a small company's capability, competency, credit, integrity, perseverance and tenacity to perform a specific government contract. If a Federal contracting officer proposes to reject the bid of a small business firm which is a low bidder because he questions the firm's ability to perform the contract on any of the above grounds, the case is referred to SBA. SBA personnel then contact the company concerned to inform it of the impending decision, and to offer an opportunity to apply to SBA for a **Certificate of Competency (COC)**, which, if granted, would require award of the contract to the firm in accordance with the Small Business Act.

SBA may also, at its discretion, issue a COC in connection with the sale of Federal property if the responsibility (capacity, credit, integrity, tenacity and perseverance) of the purchaser is questioned, and for firms found ineligible by a contracting officer due to a provision of the Walsh-Healey Public Contracts Act which requires that a government contractor be either a manufacturer or a regular dealer.

Contact: Office of Industrial Assistance, Small Business Administration, 8th Floor, 409 3rd Street SW, Washington, DC 20416. Phone (202) 205-6475.

For More Information on Selling to Specific Agencies

Department of Agriculture

Procurement procedures are explained in *Selling to USDA*. This publication contains information on who does the buying, the types of items bought for the various programs, and where the buying is done. Included is a directory of purchasing offices and their locations.

Copies are available from: Department of Agriculture, Procurement Division, Room 1550, South Bldg., Washington, DC 20215. Phone (202) 720-7527.

Department of Commerce

Procurement procedures are explained in *How to Sell to the Department of Commerce*. This publication contains information on who-buys-what-where. Included is a directory of purchasing offices and their locations.

Copies are available from: General Procurement Division, Department of Commerce, 14th & Constitution Avenue NW, Room H6516, Washington, DC 20230. Phone (202) 377-5555.

Department of Energy

The Procurement Operations Office handles acquisitions, grants, cooperative agreements, loan guarantees and other financial assistance instruments, management and operating contracts, personal property management, sales contracts, small business/small disadvantaged business/labor surplus area acquisitions, and other business activities.

The procurement procedures of the Department are explained in *Doing Business with the Department of Energy.* This publication contains information on who does the buying, the

Procurement Data - std. report

Fed. Equip. Data Center

Potential Contr. Program — fax ^{pd.} 72-73

Dept. of Energy - pg 28 - fax

1-202- 708-0294 call back
michelle ~9 AM

HUD - pg 25

Co. NAME
Address
~ fax #

(202)

401
-1546

types of items, and where the buying is done. Included is a directory of purchasing offices and their locations.

Copies are available from: Department of Energy, Procurement and Assistance Management Directorate, Code: MA 451, 1000 Independence Avenue SW, Washington, DC 20585. Phone (202) 586-1370.

Department of Housing and Urban Development

Doing Business with HUD explains HUD's mission, major programs and the procurement opportunities it creates, both directly through HUD and indirectly through State and local governments and other organizations which receive financial assistance from the Department.

Also included is a brief description of HUD's procurement procedures, a directory of purchasing offices, and an explanation of HUD's Procurement Opportunity Programs for minority, women-owned businesses.

Copies are available from: Procurement and Contracts Office, Department of Housing and Urban Development, Room 5260, 451 Seventh Street SW, Washington, DC 20410. Phone (202) 708-1290.

Environmental Protection Agency

The procurement procedures are explained in *Doing Business with EPA*. This booklet will aid a business in its efforts to acquire contract work with EPA. It contains information on contact points, addresses and telephone numbers of contracting offices, and describes the types of products and services generally acquired of EPA.

Contact: Environmental Protection Agency, Washington, DC 20460. Phone (202) 260-9426.

Department of the Treasury

The procurement procedures are explained in *Selling to the Department of the Treasury*. This publication contains information on who does the buying, the types of items bought for the various programs, and where the buying is done. Included is a directory of purchasing offices and their locations.

Copies are available from Department of Treasury, Room 6100 Treasury Annex, Washington, DC 20220. Phone (202) 566-9616.

Veterans Administration

Request *Could You Use a Multibillion Dollar Customer?* which has everything you need to know about this lucrative market.

Contact: Procurement and Supply Services Office, Veterans Administration, 810 Vermont Avenue NW, Washington, DC 20420. Phone (202) 233-3054.

Chapter 6

Everything You Ever Wanted To Know, But Were Ashamed To Ask (Or, Questions That Would Make Dr. Ruth Blush)

Customized Economic Research

Customized data is available from an economic model designed to measure the impacts of private sector developments and of government programs. Some of the variables included are output, employment, wage rates, population, government revenues, retail sales, investment, and labor force. The model can be used to analyze regional distribution of policy or economic impacts. It assures that the sum of regional activities is consistent with forecasts of national activity.

Businesses can also obtain special data showing the economic effects of potential projects on specific regions. The system offers estimates of economic impact multipliers for 500 industries for any county or group of counties in the United States.

Some examples of the use of the Regional Input-Output Modeling System include: determination of the effect that new warehouse construction would have on personal earnings, assessing the employment effects of various types of urban redevelopment expenditures, the economic impact of port facility expansion, or the effects of new plants on regional private-sector economic activity.

Contact: Bureau of Economic Analysis, Department of Commerce, Room BE61, 1401 K Street, NW, Washington, DC 20230. Phone Dr. John Kort at (202) 523-0591 for state and national impact and phone Richard Beemiller, (202) 523-0594 for analysis by county.

Correct in Every Weigh

The **Weights and Measures Office** provides leadership and technical resources to assure that commercial weights and measures are accurate and that quantity statements on packages are correct. It promotes a uniform national weights and measures system and sponsors the **National Conference on Weights and Measures** as a national forum for the promotion of uniformity and effectiveness in state and local weights and measures programs.

Data is prepared and distributed on weights and measures units, systems, and equivalents for use by Federal, state and local governments, educational institutions, business and industry, and the general public.

Contact: Weights and Measures Office, National Institute of Standards and Technology (formerly National Bureau of Standards), Department of Commerce, Room A-617, Gaithersburg, MD 20899. Phone (301) 975-4005.

Business Statistics 24 Hours a Day, 365 Days a Year

Four special telephone lines allow businesses to call any hour of the day to get recorded information on major economic statistics. The index of leading indicators recording includes the levels and percentage changes for the latest three months for the leading indicators. Also included are the contribution that changes in each of the dozen statistical series made to the overall index.

Another recording carries information on two other quarterly statistics, merchandise trade on a balance of payments basis and U.S. international transactions.

A third number handles the Gross National Product figures.

Details of personal income and outlays are available on the fourth telephone line.

Call (202) 898-2450 for a recording of the leading indicator statistics; 898-2451 for gross national product statistics; 898-2452 for personal income and outlay statistics, and 898-2953 for merchandise trade or U.S. international transactions.

If you need to write them, it's: Bureau of Economic Analysis, Department of Commerce, Room BE-53, 1401 K Street NW, Washington, DC 20230.

Using Census Data to Locate Your Business or Customers

Owners and operators of small businesses often find statistics from the Census Bureau to be of value in such activities as selecting the best location for a new store, deciding on target areas for advertising, determining an appropriate share of the market, and assessing business competition. Census statistics contribute to planning and decision making in these activities through helping business people determine how many potential customers there are in an area, what the dollar value of sales is in merchandise lines of interest to them, what volume of business is done by specific types of businesses, and the answers to related questions.

Included in Census Bureau reports are statistics showing the number of people in defined areas by age, race, sex, occupation, income, and other characteristics; the number of households and selected housing information, including housing value and rent; business activity and industrial production; imports/exports, and other useful information.

Data from the censuses are generally presented for cities, metropolitan areas, counties, states, regions, and the nation. In addition, the Census of Population and Housing is the source of data for much smaller areas, such as city blocks and census tracts (small areas roughly equivalent to neighborhoods).

Contact: Bureau of the Census, Department of Commerce, Customer Service Branch, Washington, DC 20233. Phone (301) 763-4100. Regional Census offices also may be contacted for assistance.

Federal Help on Automating Your Business

A critical element of the U.S. industrial base, both civilian and military, is the 130,000 small manufacturing firms which have traditionally supplied 70% of the component parts to our largest manufacturers. They are under intense competitive pressure from overseas suppliers.

The elements of that competition they must contend with are:

● world-class quality.

● price.

● just-in-time delivery.

● rapid response to changing market needs and new technologies.

The challenges small manufacturing businesses face are that:

● most do not truly understand that they are competing in global markets.

● they do not know about off-the-shelf Flexible Computer Integrated Manufacturing (FCIM) systems which offer one key potential solution. FCIM provides

small batch production of a wide variety of products,
with almost no down time, with the same per-unit cost
for batches of 1 or 1,000.

- many small firm owners are not computer literate and
  so are afraid of FCIM.

- the cost can be prohibitive for an individual firm
  attempting to adopt FCIM.

- most CEOs do not know how to manage a firm using
  FCIM as a tool.

To help small firms cope with these problems, the
Department of Commerce's Office of Productivity,
Technology, and Innovation developed a business
financing/management/transition technique called shared
FCIM. This consists of a manufacturing service center which
has state-of-the-art/off-the-shelf Flexible Manufacturing
Systems (FMS) systems that lease manufacturing time to
small firms.

This is the same technique used by mainframe computer
manufacturers to introduce computers to the business
community in the 1950s. However, it became clear that
retraining of management and work, whether it was leased or
used in-house, that the business aspects FCIM must be
understood.

The result was the development of the "Teaching Factory"
which combines the manufacturing service center and a
comprehensive educational component for management and
work force.

The resulting benefits include: immediate competitive
manufacturing capability with no large up-front costs,
strategic planning for the appropriate degree of automation,
training of management and work force before making an
investment, testing of systems to assure they meet individual
firm needs and fast utilization of capacity when firms install
their own equipment.

A short mention of the program in the *Kiplinger Washington Letter* resulted in 450 requests for information. Based on the projections of the centers beginning implementation or planning some 200 shared FCIMs are envisioned in the next decade.

Key points to remember are that:

- Flexible manufacturing automation may well be critical to the survival of many domestic small manufacturing businesses.

- Only a small percentage of small firms have begun to automate—most without a long-term strategy.

- Management understanding of the true **business impact** of automation is key to its **adoption** and **effective use**.

Contact: Office of Technology Commercialization, U.S. Department of Commerce, Room 4418, Washington, D.C. 20230. Phone Theodore J. Lettes at (202) 377-8111.

Manufacturing Centers

The Manufacturing Technology Centers Program helps small- and medium-size companies implement automated manufacturing technology. The **National Institute of Standards and Technology** provides planning and operating funds to the centers, along with participation in cooperative exchanges of modern technology. Advanced manufacturing techniques and methods for fostering their use that are successful at one center are generally available for use in the centers and businesses throughout the nation.

Contact: Manufacturing Technology Centers Program, National Institute of Standards and Technology (formerly National Bureau of Standards), Department of Commerce, Building 221, Room A363, Gaithersburg, MD 20899. Phone (301) 975-5020.

Flexible Manufacturing Systems Program

This program provides basic data on concepts related to financing methods and organizational structures that can make automation a realistic option for small- and medium-sized manufacturers. Information is provided on computer-integrated manufacturing, and especially on automated, flexible manufacturing systems. They will consult with you on your problem.

Contact: Flexible Manufacturing Systems Program, Office of Productivity, Technology and Innovation, Department of Commerce, 14th & E Street NW, Room 4814B, Washington, DC 20230. Phone (202) 377-1093.

Easy Access to Price and Cost Data

Information is available which helps evaluate consumer, producer, export, and import prices and price changes. **The Bureau of Labor Statistics** provides the actual data and assistance in using this data for two major economic indexes: the consumer price index (CPI) and the producer price index (PPI).

A series of regularly issued publications is prepared by this office. The major titles are *Consumer Price Index*, *Producer Price Index*, *Export Price Index*, and *Import Price Index*.

Recorded messages offer:

- General CPI and employment data (202) 523-9658

- Detailed CPI data (202) 523-1239; Detailed produce price data (202) 523-1765.

Contact: Bureau of Labor Statistics, Department of Labor, 600 E Street NW, Room 3205, Washington, DC 20212. For other help, call (202) 272-5038.

Productivity Indexes For Your Industry

Indexes of productivity for more than 150 industries are published each year. The factors underlying productivity movements also are carried out. Comparison of U.S. and foreign productivity are available. Comparative productivity measures for the total economy and the iron and steel industry and other labor economic indicators—hourly compensation costs, unit labor costs, prices, employment and unemployment, industrial dispute activity, and other selected measures are prepared.

Employment and occupational implications of technological change and technological changes emerging among selected American industries and the technological innovations such as computers are available. In addition, in-depth studies including data on dissemination of technology are prepared periodically for selected major industries where significant changes are taking place on a large scale.

Contact: Bureau of Labor Statistics, Department of Labor, Francis Perkins Building S-4325, 200 Constitution Avenue NW, Washington, DC 20210. Phone Edward Dean at (202) 523-9294.

Finding Out How You Compare with The Competition

The **Interfirm Productivity Comparisons** (IPC) program is a method for a group of managers of competing firms in the same industry to receive confidential productivity report cards based on a set of approximately 30 critical operating and financial ratios. Participants also receive numerical class ranks describing how their firm compares with competitors.

In addition, organizations sponsoring interfirm comparisons projects (e.g. trade associations) are given summary analyses useful for policy or program initiatives in behalf of the industry.

The **Office of Technology Commercialization** offers technical assistance, explanations of the concept, and basic information a prospective user needs before undertaking an **Interfirm Productivity Comparison**. This OPTI service is provided to groups of companies principally through such intermediary vehicles as trade associations.

Contact: Interfirm Productivity Comparisons Program, Office of Technology Commercialization, Department of Commerce, Room 4418, 14th & E Street NW, Washington, DC 20230. Phone (202) 377-2922.

Information on Radio, TV and Telecommunications

The office of **Policy Analysis and Development** will assist businesses in locating information or assistance concerning the deregulation of telecommunications industries, the telephone industry, radio and television broadcasting, and cable television. It also assists in linking businesses to appropriate telecommunications contacts.

Contact: Office of Policy Analysis and Development, National Telecommunications and Information Administration, Department of Commerce, 14th & Constitution Avenue NW, Room 4725, Washington, DC 20230. Phone (202) 377-1800.

Make Use of Federal Computerized Information Searches

Information searches tailored for your needs are available from the **Industrial Applications Centers**. Two types of literature searches are offered:

- Retrospective Searches identify published or unpublished literature. Results are screened and documents identified according to a client's interest profile. Results are tailored to specific needs. Backup reports identified in a search usually are available upon request.

- Current Awareness Searches provide selected weekly, monthly, or quarterly abstracts on new developments in any selected area of interest. Companies will receive printouts automatically.

Technical assistance is also available. IAC engineers will help evaluate the results of these literature searches. They can find answers to technical problems and put clients in touch with scientists and engineers at appropriate NASA Field Centers.

Prospective clients can obtain more information about these services by contacting the nearest Center. User fees are charged for their information services. The eight centers are:

- Aerospace Research Applications Center, Indianapolis Center for Advanced Research, 611 N. Capitol Avenue, Indianapolis, IN 46204. Phone (317) 262-5003.

- Kerr Industrial Applications Center, Southeastern Oklahoma State University, Station A, Box 2584, Durant, OK 74701. Phone (405) 924-6822.

- NASA Industrial Applications Center, 823 William Pitt Union, University of Pittsburgh, Pittsburgh, PA 15260. Phone (412) 624-5211.

- NASA Industrial Applications Center, University of Southern California, Denney Research Building, Los Angeles, CA 90007. Phone (213) 743-6132.

- NASA-Florida State Technology Applications Center, University of Florida, 307 Weil Hall, Gainesville, FL 32611. Phone (904) 392-6760.

- NASA/UK Technology Applications Program, University of Kentucky, 109 Kinkead Hall, Lexington, KY 40506. Phone (606) 257-6322.

- NASA/RMS, P.O. Box 8757, BWI Airport, MD, 21090. Phone (301) 621-0100.

- New England Research Applications Center, Mansfield Professional Park, Storrs, CT 06268. Phone (203) 486-4533.

Questions about Standards, Specifications, Test Methods, and Nomenclature

The **National Center for Standards and Certification Information** maintains a reference collection on more than 240,000 standards, specifications, test methods, certification rules, codes, nomenclature, and recommended practices.

They can answer questions such as:

- Are there standards for electric toasters?

- Have test methods been established for characteristics of bricks?

- Has nomenclature for quality control been defined?

- Have specifications for magnetic ink been established?

They can answer the same questions for some foreign countries, or can refer you to the right person.

A newsletter is published on proposed U.S. or foreign regulations that may affect U.S. manufacturers.

Contact: National Center for Standards and Certification Information, Room A-163, TRF Building, National Institute of Standards and Technology (formerly Bureau of Standards), Gaithersburg, MD 20899. Phone (301) 975-4040.

Assistance for Energy-related Projects

The **National Appropriate Technology Assistance Service** (NATAS) helps entrepreneurs develop energy-related projects by providing information and direct business assistance. They can help with such things as: identifying the best opportunities, acquiring financing, marketing, business planning, and organization. Technical support on inventions is also provided.

One of the more innovative aspects of NATAS is its commercialization technical assistance.

Contact: NATAS, Department of Energy, P.O. Box 2525, Butte, MT 59702. Phone George Everett at (800) 428-2525, or from within Montana (800) 428-1718.

Uncle Sam Helps Negotiate with Transportation Firms

The **Transportation Office** helps small grain cooperatives and merchandising firms negotiate rate and service conditions with railroads. The office publishes a weekly Grain Transportation Report to keep small shippers apprised of changes in grain transportation and also offers technical assistance and advice for specific transportation-related problems.

Contact: Railroad Department, Transportation Office, Department of Agriculture, 14th & Independence Avenue SW, Washington, DC 20250. Phone (202) 245-5330.

Sending Perishables Overseas

Most perishable agricultural commodities move into the export market by air or ocean transportation. **The Transportation Office** assists exporters with ocean and air freight transportation problems through a liaison with major transportation companies, shipping agencies, regulatory bodies, and foreign agricultural attaches.

Technical assistance and information is available to small businessmen who encounter export problems. Specific information on the transportation requirements for exporting produce is available in two handbooks. Tip sheets on the transportation of livestock are available. In addition, short-term applied research conducted on special problems encountered in the transport of agricultural products is available.

Contact: Export Shipping Department, Transportation Office, Department of Agriculture, 14th & Independence Avenue SW, Washington, DC 20250. Phone (202) 245-5323.

Help with Ocean Common Carriers

The **Federal Maritime Commission** provides a forum for settling disputes between carriers and shippers. The Commission will listen to informal complaints and try to bring about a voluntary settlement. If warranted, formal proceedings can be initiated for unlawful practices. They may award reparations for economic injuries from violations.

Each year they respond to over a thousand inquiries and complaints.

Contact: Office of Informal Complaints and Inquiries, Federal Maritime Commission, 1100 L Street NW, Washington, DC 20573. Phone Geoffrey Rogers, Director, at (202) 523-5807.

Truck Costs and Technical Help

Many truckers of agricultural commodities are also small businessmen in that they use their own tractor/trailer rig to haul freight for a profit. For USDA refrigerator carriers, the **Transportation Office** publishes a monthly truck cost report, which provides information on current per-mile operating costs for a typical fresh fruit and vegetable trucker. Information on this report, as well as truck costing, is available.

Contact: Truck Department, Agricultural Marketing Service, Department of Agriculture, 14th Street & Independence Avenue SW, Washington, DC 20250. Phone (202) 245-5328.

Problems to Avoid if You're Starting a Trucking Company

The **Public Assistance Office** acts as a clearinghouse and focal point for the resolution of questions and problems experienced by businesses and individuals. It provides advice and technical assistance to small businesses, minority truckers, new entrants into the transportation field, small shippers, and small carriers, and deals with other members of the general public as well.

Its chief function is to counsel small business entities and individuals in understanding and coping with the rules, regulations, policies, and procedures of the Commission. Much of this work involves assistance in obtaining operating rights—licenses to perform interstate transportation—from how to fill out the application form to complying with tariff filings and insurance requirements.

As part of its information outreach program, the office prepares and disseminates numerous booklets designed to answer some basic questions about the surface transportation industries. These include problems small businesses and individuals confront in entering the trucking business, starting a short-line railroad, and participating in rail abandonment proceedings.

The office plays a significant role in tackling and preventing transportation problems by initiating or commenting upon proposed rules or legislation relating to matters impacting upon areas of concern to small businesses.

Contact: Public Assistance Office, Interstate Commerce Commission, Washington, DC 20423. Phone (202) 275-7597.

So You Want to Start a Small Railroad

It may surprise some to find out the short-line railroad industry is experiencing a comeback. Each year, about two dozen new owners or operators are authorized to begin operation. One reason is the Interstate Commerce

Commission's refusal to burden new operators with the cost of labor-protective conditions.

Write for a copy of *So You Want To Start a Small Railroad* from the Office of Public Assistance, Interstate Commerce Commission, Washington, DC 20423, or call Fran Grimmett at (202) 275-7597.

Chapter 7

Financial Help

The Farmers Home Administration's **Business and Industrial Loan Program** guarantees up to 90% of principal and interest on loans made by commercial lenders to establish or improve businesses and industries, if they primarily are used to help preserve or create new employment opportunities for rural people. Loans may assist enterprises located in the countryside and in towns or cities of up to a population of 50,000.

The money may be used for business acquisitions, construction, conversion, enlargement, repair, purchasing land, easements, buildings, equipment and supplies.

The FmHA has fewer rules than the SBA; for example, the FmHA will consider loans for publishing enterprises and the SBA will (usually) not.

Contact: Farmers Home Administration, Department of Agriculture, 14th & Independence Avenue SW, Washington, DC 20250. Phone (202) 447-4100.

Loans for Teenagers

Youth Project Loans from the **Farmers Home Administration** are available to youngsters ages 10 through 20 in rural communities. They will finance nearly any kind of income-producing project. Kids have started landscaping companies, repair shops, catering services, roadside stands and art/crafts sales enterprises, among others. The money can be used for equipment, supplies, renting tools, buying livestock, and for operating expenses. Only small projects are financed.

Contact: Youth Project Loans, Farmers Home Administration, 14th & Independence Avenue SW, Washington, DC 20250. For a pamphlet describing the program call
(202) 382-1632.

Nonfarm Enterprises on Farms

The **Farmers Home Administration** makes loans and gives technical and management assistance for businesses to supplement farm income. They can make loans up to $200,000 and guarantee bank loans up to $400,000. These loans have financed welding shops, service stations, grocery stores, barber shops, cabinetmakers, sporting goods stores, beauty shops, riding stables, repair services, and restaurants, among others.

Applications of veterans receive preference. To be eligible one must be or intend to become the owner-operator of a family-sized farm or be a tenant on such a farm.

The loans may be used for buildings, land, buying or renting tools and equipment, furnishings, operating expenses, refinance debts, pay closing costs, purchase inventories or supplies, pay for organizing the enterprise, develop water and waste disposal systems for the enterprise and construct necessary roads.

Contact: Farmers Home Administration, 14th & Independence Avenue SW, Washington, DC 20250. Phone

(202) 447-3889 and ask for the Nonfarm Enterprise Loan pamphlet.

A Potpourri of Farmers Home Administration Loans

The FmHA has loan programs for purchasing and developing farms, buying livestock and equipment, paying farm and home operating equipment, converting farms to outdoor recreation enterprises, constructing buildings and homes, providing rental housing, developing water and waste disposal systems, refinancing debts, and soil and water conservation.

Contact: Farmers Home Administration, Department of Agriculture, 14th & Independence Avenue SW, Washington, DC 20250. Phone (202) 447-4323.

If You Have a Low Income or Have Been Denied Financing

If you have a low income, are located in a high unemployment area *or* have been denied financing despite ability to repay, the Small Business Administration may have a loan for you. Funds may be used to construct, expand or convert facilities, purchase equipment, or for working capital. In 1992 approximately 3,000,000,000 dollars will be available to fourteen thousand applicants thru direct loans or loan guarantees. Direct loans range up to $150,000, guarantees up to $750,000.

Ask for information on the 7(a) and 7(a)(11) programs.

Contact: Director, Office of Business Loans, Small Business Administration, 1441 L Street NW, Washington, DC 20416. Phone (202) 205-6490.

Small Business Administration Loans

The Small Business Administration offers a variety of loan programs, the agency provides guaranteed and direct loans to small businesses to help them finance plant construction, conversion or expansion. The loans can also be used to acquire equipment, facilities and supplies. Most assistance is provided through SBA loan guarantees, provided by private lenders (bank and non-bank lenders) to eligible small business concerns which cannot borrow on reasonable terms from conventional lenders without government help. Loan guarantees carry a maximum of $750,000. SBA can guarantee up to 90 percent of a loan, depending on the loan amount. Maturity may be up to 25 years. The average size of a guaranteed business loan is $175,000 and the average maturity is about eight years.

Special Loan Programs

- **Contract Loans** to assist small firms with short-term financing. Loan proceeds can be used to finance labor and materials, not to exceed the term of the contract or 18 months. This is not a revolving line of credit, each loan must be paid in full at the end of each contract.

- **Seasonal Line of Credit Guarantees** to provide short-term financing for small firms having a seasonal loan requirement due to seasonal increase in business activity.

- **Small General Contractors Loans** to assist small construction firms with short-term financing. Loan proceeds can be used to finance residential or commercial construction or rehabilitation of property for sale. Proceeds cannot be used for owning and operating real estate for investment purposes.

- **Small Loan Program** to meet the ever growing need for loans of $50,000 or less, the SBA initiated the program. It is anticipated that these loans will be of particular value to small firms in the service sector. A new and simplified application form (SBA Form 4

Short Form) has been designed by SBA to facilitate use of the Small Loan Program.

There are fact sheets available describing these programs from your local SBA office or by calling (800) 827-5722.

Contact: Small Business Administration, Suite 800, 409 3rd Street SW, Washington, DC 20416. Phone (202) 205-6450

Loan Guarantees for Agricultural Exports

The **Export Credit Guarantee Program** (GSM-102) run by the **Agriculture Department's Commodity Credit Corporation** is designed to expand U.S. agricultural exports by stimulating U.S. bank financing of foreign purchases on credit terms of up to three years. In every transaction the foreign buyer's bank must issue an irrevocable letter of credit covering the port value of the commodity exported.

The **Credit Corporation's** guarantee will cover most of the amount owed to the U.S. bank in case the foreign bank defaults. The program operates in situations where credit is necessary to increase or maintain U.S. exports to a foreign market and where private financial institutions would be unwilling to provide financing without guarantee.

A secondary objective is to permit some countries with improved financial conditions to purchase on fully commercial terms.

The **Intermediate Export Credit Guarantee** program (GSM-103) is similar but provides coverage on credit terms in excess of three but not greater than ten years.

Under these programs, guarantee coverage may be made available on credits extended for freight cost and marine and war risk insurance costs associated with U.S. agricultural exports. The **Credit Corporation** announces availability of such coverage on a case-by-case basis.

Contact: Foreign Agricultural Service, Commodity Credit Corporation, Department of Agriculture, 14th &

Independence Avenue SW, Washington, DC 20250. Phone
(202) 447-3224 or 447-3573.

Grants for Inventions

The **Energy-Related Inventions Office** encourages
innovation in non-nuclear energy technology by helping
individual inventors and small R&D companies to develop
promising energy-related inventions. It evaluates all
submitted inventions and recommends those that are
promising, to the Department of Energy (DOE).

The evaluation criteria are: technical feasibility, degree of
energy impact, commercial potential, and intrinsic technical
merit. DOE then reviews the recommended inventions and,
working closely with the inventor, determines the next
reasonable step for the invention and how much money it
will take. Most often, support takes the form of a
one-time-only cash grant and technical assistance in
developing linkages with the private sector.

Contact: Energy-Related Inventions Office, National Institute
of Standards and Technology, Department of Commerce,
Building 411, Room A115, Gaithersburg, MD 20899. Phone
(301) 975-5500.

Funds for Fishing

The **Commercial Fisheries Financial Assistance Programs**
include the:

- **Fisheries Obligation Guarantee Program** which
  provides a Federal Guarantee of financing of
  commercial fishing vessels and shoreside facilities.

- Capital Construction Fund Program which defers
  Federal income taxes for agreement holders on
  commercial fishing operations to permit accumulation
  of capital for use in approved commercial fishing
  vessel acquisition or reconstruction projects.

Contact: National Oceanic and Atmospheric Administration, National Marine Fisheries Service, Department of Commerce, Financial Services Division, F/TWI, 1335 East West Highway, Silver Spring, MD 20910. Phone (301) 427-2393.

If Your Fishing Boat or Gear is Destroyed

If your fishing boat is destroyed by a foreign vessel or if your fishing gear is damaged by an oil-related activity, the government may make direct payments to you from one of the following programs;

● **Boat Destruction**

In 1991, approximately 150 claims for fishing boat destruction totaling $1,000,000 were paid. The claims ranged from $600 to $150,000.

The applicant must be a U.S. commercial fisherman and a U.S. citizen. The incident must have occurred within the U.S. Fishery Conservation zone or in an area where the United States has exclusive management authority. You need to keep affidavits, receipts, log books, and inventories to show you're a fisherman and owned the property for which compensation is claimed.

● **Gear Loss**

If you lost gear because of an oil- or gas-related activity in any area of the outer Continental Shelf, the government will pay for the gear plus 50% of the resulting economic loss.

In 1990 approximately 126 claims for gear damage, ranging from $500 to $25,000, were paid, totaling $700,000.

There are no restrictions on the use of these funds.

You must present financial statements, receipts, log books, and affidavits to establish you are a fisherman and owned the equipment for which compensation is claimed.

Contact: Financial Services Division, Attn: National Marine Fisheries Service, Department of Commerce, 1335 East West Highway, Silver Spring, MD 20910. Phone (301) 427-2390.

If Your Fishing Boat Is Seized

The **Department of State** will reimburse you if your fishing boat is seized by a foreign country on the high seas.

In addition, if the seizure occurs in waters claimed by the foreign country as territorial, but the claim is not recognized by the United States, the State Department will still pay.

Pre-registration and payment of a premium fee are necessary.

Losses payable are limited to the market value of the fish before seizure, market value of the boat and gear, and 50% of the gross income lost.

In 1990, 45 claims totaling $1,600,000 were paid. Whether or not you pre-register, the government will reimburse you for fines paid to a foreign government to secure the release of your boat.

Contact: Office of Fisheries Affairs, Bureau of Oceans and International Environmental and Scientific Affairs, Room 5806, Department of State, Washington, D.C. 20520-7818. Phone Stetson Tinkham at (202) 647-2009.

Minority Loans for Department of Energy Research

The **Minority Loan Program** was established to assist minority business enterprises in participating fully in DOE research, development, demonstration and contract activities. The financial assistance is in the form of direct loans, whereby DOE will provide funds to a minority business borrower from its appropriated funds.

The loans are to assist a minority business borrower in financing up to 75% of costs a borrower incurs in preparing a bid or proposal to attempt to obtain DOE contracts or agreements.

The maximum amount of money that can be borrowed for any one loan is $50,000.

Contact: Minority Economic Impact Office, Department of Energy, 1000 Independence Avenue SW, Room 5B-110, Washington, DC 20585. Phone (202) 586-1594.

Financing of Architectural and Engineering Overseas Projects

The **Export-Import Bank (Eximbank)** provides financing to help U.S. architectural and engineering firms win foreign contracts for project-related feasibility studies and pre-construction engineering services. Under the program, **Eximbank**, the U.S. Government agency charged with facilitating financing for U.S. exports, offers medium-term loans directly to the foreign purchasers of those services, and guarantees private financing for a portion of the local costs of the project.

To qualify for the program, the contract must involve a project with the potential to generate additional U.S. exports worth $10,000,000 or twice the amount of the initial contract, whichever is greater.

Contact: Export-Import Bank of the United States, 811 Vermont Avenue NW, Washington, DC 20571. Phone toll-free (800) 424-5201; firms in Alaska, Hawaii and Washington DC should call (202) 566-8860.

Insurance on Credit to Foreigners

American companies often find that extending credit to foreign buyers is essential to expand or win business. But distance, unfamiliar legal procedures and unforeseen political or economic events make credit sales to foreign buyers riskier than similar sales to domestic customers.

Eximbank's Policies, offered through its agent, the **Foreign Credit Insurance Association** (FCIA), makes it easier for companies, even those with little or no exporting experience, to get credit risk protection for their export credit sales.

Four policies are offered:

- The **Umbrella Policy** enables state and local government agencies, banks, export trading companies, freight forwarders and other financial and professional organizations to become administrators of short-term credit risk insurance covering the export sales of numerous exporters. These administrators assume responsibility for collecting premiums, reporting shipments, filling out forms and processing claims on behalf of the exporters insured under their **Umbrella Policy**.

  This policy gives new exporters greater access to foreign credit risk protection and lessens their paperwork burdens. It also helps exporters get financing because the policy proceeds are assignable to any financial institution as collateral on a hold harmless basis. Administrators of Umbrella Policies benefit as well. The Umbrella Policy enables them to offer an important service to their small- and medium-sized business customers.

- The **New-to-Export Policy** assists companies which are just beginning to export or have an annual export sales volume of less than $750,000.

- The **Short-Term Multi-Buyer Policy** is available for any exporter.

- The **Bank-to-Bank Letter of Credit Policy** is available to any bank financing export sales on an irrevocable letter of credit basis.

Products and services include consumables, raw materials, spare parts, agricultural commodities, capital goods, consumer durables and services.

Contact: Export-Import Bank of the United States, 811 Vermont Avenue, NW, Washington, DC 20571. Phone toll-free (800) 424-5201; firms in Alaska, Hawaii and Washington DC should call (202) 566-4490.

Fixed Rate Loans for Exports

Eximbank offers a wide range of financial support programs, including loans and guarantees of loans made by others. The loan and guarantee programs cover up to 85% of the U.S. export value, with repayment on each transaction it supports. Creditworthiness of the buyer, the buyer's country and the exporter's ability to perform are considered.

Eximbank's loans provide competitive, fixed interest rate financing for U.S. export sales facing foreign competition backed by subsidized financing from another government. Evidence of such competition is not required for exports produced by small businesses where the loan amount is $2,500,000 or less.

Eximbank extends direct loans to foreign buyers of U.S. exports and intermediary loans to fund responsible parties who agree to on lend to foreign buyers. Eximbank's interest rates follow the guidelines of the export credit arrangement among the members of the Organization for Economic Cooperation and Development (OECD).

Eximbank's guarantees provide repayment protection for private sector loans to creditworthy foreign buyers of U.S. goods and services. Eximbank's guarantees are available alone or may be combined with an intermediary loan. Most guarantees provide comprehensive protection for both political and commercial risks.

Contact: Export-Import Bank of the United States, 811 Vermont Avenue, NW, Washington, DC 20571. Phone (800)

424-5201, firms in Alaska, Hawaii, and Washington DC
should call (202) 566-4490.

Get a Revolving Line of Credit for Exports

The (ERLC) was established to help more small businesses
export their products and services abroad. Through this
program SBA can guarantee up to 85% of a bank line of
credit (up to a maximum of $750,000) to a small business
exporter. (On amounts under $155,000 SBA can guarantee up
to 90% of the loan.) Any number of withdrawals and
repayments can be made as long as the dollar limit of the line
is not exceeded and the repayments are made within the
stated maturity period, generally not to exceed 12 months
(although, in certain cases, maturities may extend to 36
months).

Though proceeds need not be used exclusively for pre-export
purposes, loan proceeds are generally used to finance labor
or materials needed for manufacturing or to purchase goods
or services for export. Proceeds may also be used to develop
foreign markets or to finance accounts receivable.

Applicants must qualify as small under SBA size standards
and meet the other eligibility requirements for all SBA loans.
In addition, the applicant should have been in business (not
necessarily in exporting) for at least 12 months prior to filing
an application; however, where management displays
sufficient export trade experience to warrant an exception,
this requirement may be waived.

If a loan request exceeds SBA's loan guaranty limit of
$750,000, a co-guaranty with the United States
Export-Import Bank should be considered.

ERLC loans are available only under SBA's **Guaranty Plan**.
A prospective applicant should review the export financing
needs of the business with their bank. If the bank is unable or
unwilling to make the loan directly, the possibilities of a
participation with SBA should be explored. The participation
of a private lender is necessary in order to consummate
an ERLC.

Contact: Export Revolving Line of Credit Loan Program (ERLC), Small Business Administration, 409 3rd Street SW, Washington, DC 20416. Phone (202) 205-6497.

International Trade Loan Program

The **International Trade Loan Program** helps small businesses that are engaged or preparing to engage in international trade, as well as those adversely affected by competition from imports, to acquire or modernize facilities or equipment that will be used in the production of goods or services within the United States. SBA can guarantee up to $1,000,000 for facilities or equipment and $250,000 for working capital.

Contact the SBA district office nearest you, or U.S. Small Business Administration, Office of Financial Assistance, 409 Third Street, SW, Washington, DC 20416.

Another Source of Export Loan Guarantees

The **SBA-EXIM Co-Guarantee Program** provides for co-guarantees to small business exporters and export trading companies. The co-guarantees extends to loans in principal amounts ranging from $200,000 to $1,000,000 on a per-borrower basis and covers 85% of the loan amount.

The terms and conditions of co-guarantees, except where otherwise provided, are determined by SBA rules and regulations for **Export Revolving Line of Credit** (ERLC) loans.

Proceeds may be used only to finance labor and materials needed for manufacturing or wholesaling for export, and to penetrate or develop foreign markets.

Contact: Small Business Administration, 409 3rd Street SW, Washington, DC 20416.

More Loan Guarantees, Including Insurance for Exporters

The Overseas Private Investment Corporation (a government agency) offers the **Contractors and Exporters Program** to improve the competitive position of American contractors and exporters seeking to do business in the developing nations. OPIC offers specialized insurance and financing services.

Many developing countries require foreign firms to post bid, performance or advance payment guarantees in the form of standby letters of credit when bidding on or performing overseas contracts. OPIC's political risk insurance for contractors and exporters protects against the arbitrary or unfair drawing of such letters of credit.

In addition, contractors and exporters may obtain insurance against the risks of;

- currency inconvertibility

- confiscation of tangible assets and bank accounts

- war, revolution, insurrection and civil strife

- losses sustained when a government owner fails to settle a dispute in accordance with the provisions of the underlying contract.

OPIC also offers a special loan guaranty program for small business contractors to assist with their credit needs. This plan provides an OPIC guaranty of up to 75% of a stand-by letter of credit that is issued to a financial institution on behalf of a small-business contractor.

Contact: Overseas Private Investment Corporation, 1615 M Street NW, Washington, DC 20527. Phone toll-free (800) 424-6742; for businesses within Washington, DC call (202) 457-7010.

Working Capital Guarantees for Exporters

Exporting is an important opportunity for many American companies. Sometimes, however, small- and medium-sized businesses have trouble obtaining the working capital they need to produce and market goods and services for sale abroad.

Despite their credit worthiness, these potential exporters find commercial banks and other lenders reluctant to offer them working capital financing. Some companies have already reached the borrowing limits set for them by their banks.

Others do not have the type or amount of collateral their banks require. That's why the **Export-Import Bank** of the United States developed the program. **Eximbank** does not lend to exporters directly. Instead, it encourages commercial banks and other lenders to make working capital loans by guaranteeing that, in the event of default by the exporter, Eximbank will repay most of the loan.

For more information ask about the **Working Capital Guarantee Program**.

Contact: Export-Import Bank of the United States, 811 Vermont Avenue NW, Washington, DC 20571. Phone toll-free (800) 424-5201; firms in Alaska, Hawaii and Washington DC should call (202) 566-8860 or 566-4490.

Money And Insurance for Investing in Overseas Ventures

American investors planning to share significantly in the equity and management of an oversea venture can often utilize OPIC's finance programs for medium- to long-term financing.

To obtain OPIC financing, the venture must be commercially and financially sound, within the demonstrated competence of the proposed management, and sponsored by an investor having a proven record of success in the same or closely-related business.

OPIC's financing commitment of a new venture may extend to, but not exceed, 50% of the total project cost. A larger participation may be considered for an expansion of a successful, existing enterprise.

Currently, OPIC provides financing to investors through two major programs. Direct loans, which are available only for ventures sponsored by, or significantly involving, U.S. small businesses or cooperatives, and Loan guarantees, which are available to all businesses regardless of size.

OPIC will issue a guaranty under which funding can be obtained from a variety of U.S. financial institutions. The guaranty covers both commercial and political risks.

While private investors generally have the capability to assess the commercial aspects of doing business overseas, they may be hesitant to undertake long-term investments abroad, given the political uncertainties of many developing nations. To alleviate these uncertainties, OPIC insures U.S. investments against three major types of political risks.

Inconvertibility coverage protects an investor against the inability to convert into U.S. dollars the local currency received as profits, earnings, or return of capital on an investment. OPIC's inconvertibility coverage also protects against adverse discriminatory exchange rates.

Expropriation protects the investor not only against classic nationalization of enterprises or the taking of property, but also a variety of situations which might be described as 'creeping expropriation.'

Coverage also is provided against political violence for loss due to bellicose actions (war, revolution, insurrection) and politically-motivated civil strife.

Contact: Overseas Private Investment Corporation, 1615 M Street NW, Washington, DC 20527. Phone toll-free (800) 424-6742; for businesses in Washington, DC, call (202)457-7010.

Loans for the Handicapped and for Veterans

Handicapped people and Vietnam and disabled vets unable to obtain financing in the private credit marketplace may be eligible, first, for a guaranteed/insured loan or, alternatively, for a direct loan if no bank will participate in a guaranteed loan. These loans may be used to construct, expand, or convert facilities; to purchase building equipment or materials; or to provide working capital.

The borrower must meet the SBA's definition of a small business. The applicant must;

- be of good character

- show an ability to operate a business successfully

- have a significant stake in the business

- show that the business can operate on a sound financial basis.

The applicant must be prepared to provide a statement of personal history, personal financial statements, company financial statements, and summary of collateral. The loan must be of such sound value or so secured as to provide reasonable assurance of repayment.

Applications are generally filed in the SBA field office serving the territory where the applicant's business is located. Approval takes thirty to sixty days from the date of the application acceptance, depending on the type of loan. The applicant is notified by an authorization letter from the district SBA office or participating bank.

Contact: The Business Loan Office, Small Business Administration, Room 804, 409 3rd Street SW, Washington, DC 20416.

Money for Small Business Innovative Research

All Federal departments at one time or another have research money and contracts available for small business participants in this process. Pre-solicitation announcements are available periodically from the SBA. Check your nearest SBA office for dates and details. Usually a three-month lead is given between the announcement and the time a solicitation proposal must be submitted.

In accepting a Federal contract, be mindful of the fact that you have to reply to the exact specifications required, have the ability to perform according to your bid and/or contract, and have to have the fiscal liquidity to wait for payment until the responsible Federal department unravels the sometime inevitable red tape. While delays and bureaucratic nitpicking are not commonplace or intended, they can happen; however, if you can produce according to the exacting specifications, doing business with the world's largest customer can be mighty profitable.

Departments that most frequently participate in SBIR solicitations include the U.S. Departments of Commerce, Defense, Energy, Health & Human Services, and the Environmental Protection Agency.

The SBIR Program includes the following subjects most frequently:

- Drinking water treatment

- Municipal and industrial wastewater treatment and pollution control

- Biological sludge treatment for improved handling and disposal

- Solid and hazardous waste disposal

- *In situ* treatment of hazardous and toxic waste at Superfund sites

- Innovative restoration technologies removing heavy metals at Superfund sites

- Control of acid rain precursors

- Process instrumentation for improved pollution control

- Waste reduction and pollution prevention

- Oil spill prevention, cleanup and restoration technology

- Improved measurement technologies for lead detection in lead-based paints.

Requirements are changed frequently and new ones are added. Remember that all measurement indicated in proposals and projects has to be in the metric system. The 11 departments that have permanent SBIR representatives who can be consulted for particulars are the following:

Department of Agriculture
Dr. Charles F. Cleland
Director, SBIR Program
U.S. Department of Agriculture
Room 323-J, Aerospace Building
901 D Street, S W
Washington, DC 20250-2200
(202) 401-4002

Department of Commerce
Mr. James P. Maruca
Director, Office of Small and Disadvantaged Business
    Utilization
U.S. Department of Commerce
14th and Constitution Avenue, NW
HCHB, Room 6411
Washington, DC 20230
(202) 377-1472

Mr. Edward V. Tiernan
DOC SBIR Program Manager
Suitland Professional Center
SPC, Room 307
Suitland, MD 20233
(301) 763-4240

Department of Defense
Mr. Robert Wrenn
SBIR Program Manager
OSD/SADBU
U.S. Department of Defense
The Pentagon
Room 2A340
Washington, DC 20301-3061
(703) 697-1481

Department of Education
Mr. John Christensen
SBIR Program Coordinator
U.S. Department of Education
Room 602F
555 New Jersey Avenue, NW
Washington, DC 20208
(301) 353-5867

Department of Health And Human Services
Mr. Richard Clinkscales
SBIR Program Manager
Office of the Secretary
U.S. Department of Health and Human Services
Washington, DC 20201
(202) 245-7300

Department of Transportation
Dr. George Kovatch
Chief, University Research, Technology Innovation and
Programs Office (DTS-22)
U.S. Department of Transportation

Research and Special Programs Administration
Volpe National Transportation Systems Center
Kendall Square
Cambridge, MA 02141-1093
(617) 494-2051

Environmental Protection Agency

Mr. Donald F. Carey
SBIR Program Manager
Research Grants Staff (RD-675)
Office of Research and Development
Environmental Protection Agency
401 M Street, SW
Washington, DC 20460
(202) 260-7473

National Aeronautics And Space Administration

Mr. Harry Johnson
Program Director, SBIR Price - Code CR
National Aeronautics and Space Administration
Headquarters
Washington, DC 20546
(703) 271-5659

National Science Foundation

Mr. Roland Tibbetts
Mr. Ritchie Coryell
Mr. Darryl G. Gorman
SBIR Program Managers
National Science Foundation
1800 G Street, NW
Washington, DC 20550
(202) 357-7527

Nuclear Regulatory Commission

Ms. Marianne M. Riggs
SBIR Program Representative
Program management, Policy Development and Analysis Staff

U.S. Nuclear Regulatory Commission
Washington, DC 20555
(301) 492-3625

Assistance in Obtaining Capital for Small Business Innovative Research Awardees

A system is available to identify potential sources of capital that may help SBIR awardees commercialize their research and development activities. This system is a free service that provides a list of potential investors such as venture capitalists, corporations, and state government programs.

The database is searchable by technology and industry areas, thereby allowing the office to identify the sources of capital most likely to be interested in a particular company.

This system was also designed to assist SBIR awardees seeking Phase II awards which require that special consideration be given to proposals demonstrating Phase III non-Federal capital commitments.

Contact: Innovation, Research, and Technology Office, Small Business Administration, 403 3rd Street SW, Room 500, Washington, DC 20416. Phone (202) 653-6458.

Grants for Broadcasting Stations

The **Public Telecommunications Facilities Program** provides grants to assist in the planning and construction of public telecommunications facilities. Special emphasis is placed on extending public broadcasting signals to currently unserved areas. Construction grants are awarded as matching grants up to 75% of the total cost. Planning grants are awarded up to 100% of the funds necessary for planning a project.

Special consideration is given to women and minorities.

Contact: Public Telecommunications Facilities Program, National Telecommunications and Information

Administration, U.S. Department of Commerce, Washington, DC 20230. Phone Dennis Connors at (202) 377-5802.

Money for Pollution Control

Businesses may be eligible for pollution control financing if they are unable to obtain private financing on terms or at rates comparable to businesses which do not fit the SBA definition of a small business.

Loan proceeds may be used for aspects of constructing and placing into operation any eligible facility which the SBA determines is likely to prevent, reduce, abate, or control noise, air, or water pollution.

SBA has several options for the kinds of financing instruments that can be used. Lenders can also generate funds for the loans by using marketable securities such as taxable bonds and debentures within authorized loan limits. The principal is not to exceed $5,000,000.

Contact: Small Business Administration, Pollution Control Financing Staff, 409 3rd Street SW, Washington, DC 20416. Phone (202) 205-6490.

Equity Loans

Equity investments and long-term loans are available from small business investment companies (SBICs) and section 301(d) small business investment companies (301(d)s) which are privately owned firms licensed by the SBA and partly funded by the Federal government.

256 SBICs are located throughout the U.S., many of which are assisted or "leveraged" by the U.S. Small Business Administration. 133 other SBICs are licensed specifically to provide assistance to small businesses owned by socially or economically disadvantaged persons

Some SBICs seek out small businesses with new products or services because of the strong growth potential of such firms.

Some SBICs have management skilled in specific industries and focus on them in their financing.

According to SBA criteria, a firm eligible for SBIC financing must have a net worth of under $6,000,000 and a net after-tax income during the previous two years of $2,000,000 or less. To determine the size of a business, all affiliated operations of a company have to be considered.

To apply for SBIC financing requires a minimum two-step process:

- identifying a SBIC that will handle your type of financing, and

- prepare a current business plan or prospectus that includes the following seven items:
  - Identification, product or service
  - product facilities and property
  - marketing plan
  - competition
  - management and references
  - financial statements
  - a statement of the benefits you hope to gain from the financing. A directory of SBICs is available from your nearest SBA office.

Loans must be of at least five years maturity and interest rates, which are subject to negotiation, cannot exceed current ceiling. SBICs and 301(d)s generally emphasize income-generating investments, such as convertible debentures and straight long-term debt. They tend to be most active in providing growth capital to established businesses, and are active in financing high-technology, start-up enterprises.

The applicant should prepare a business plan that describes its operations, financial condition, and financing requirements—detailing information on products, new product lines, patent positions, market and competitive data, sales and distribution, key personnel, and other pertinent factors.

Your nearest SCORE office can be of help in preparing the proper business plan. See the section on SCORE, the Service Corps of Retired Executives. Note that Section 301(d) SBICs finance only socially or economically disadvantaged small business.

Contact: Small Business Administration, Investment Division, 409 3rd Street SW, Washington, DC 20416. Phone (202) 205-7589.

Save Money on Taxes, Become A Foreign Sales Corporation

A **Foreign Sales Corporation** (FSC) is a corporation that obtains an exemption on corporate taxes on a portion of the profits earned on exports or services. Usually 15% of the profits are tax-free.

There are "regular" FSCs and small FSCs; small FSCs' rules are easier to cope with.

To get a brochure on the rules and some applications call Allen Uneworth at (202) 377-5333 or write the Office of Trade Finance, U.S. Department of Commerce, International Trade Administration, Washington, DC 20230.

Starting a Federal Credit Union

The **National Credit Union Administration** will explain how to get started, help prepare the charter application, assist in start-up operations and provide depositor insurance.

For established credit unions in low-income communities, they also have direct loans.

The guidelines for eligibility are that you can start a credit union if you have an association with at least 300 members, have an employee group of 200 or more, or live in a rural community with 500 or more families. In 1987, 315 new Federal credit union charters were granted.

For more information ask for the Credit Union Information Package. Contact: National Credit Union Administration, 1776 G Street NW, Washington, DC 20456. Phone (202) 357-1000.

Economic Injury Disaster Loans

The **Disaster Assistance Division** of the Small Business Administration can help if your business concern suffers economic injury as a result of natural disasters. If the business was within the disaster area, see the next entry, Physical Disaster Loans.

In 1990, 1951 of these loans were made for $100,000,000. The terms are up to thirty years for repayment with a $500,000 limit.

The funds are for paying current liabilities which the small concern could have paid if the disaster had not occurred. Working capital for a limited period can be provided to continue operations until conditions return to normal.

For more information request the pamphlet *Economic Injury Disaster Loans for Small Business.*

Contact: Disaster Assistance Division, Small Business Administration, 409 3rd Street SW, Washington, DC 20416. Phone (202) 653-6879.

Physical Disaster Loans

The **Disaster Assistance Division** of the Small Business Administration can help if your business is physically damaged by a natural disaster such as a hurricane, flood, or tornado. If your business is not physically damaged, but suffers economically, see the preceding section, Economic Injury Disaster Loans.

In 1990, 50,000 loans were made for $1,100,000,000. In general the terms are for thirty years, with a limit of

$500,000, although if high unemployment will result, the amount can be higher. The SBA will establish an on-site office to help with processing and disbursement.

For more information request the pamphlet *Physical Disaster Loans.*

Contact: Disaster Assistance Division, Small Business Administration, 409 3rd Street SW, Washington, DC 20416. Phone (202) 653-6879.

If You Need a Performance Bond and Can't Get One

Small contractors may find, for whatever reasons, bonding unavailable to them. If so, the Small Business Administration is authorized to guarantee to a qualified surety up to 90% of losses incurred under bid, payment, or performance bonds issued to contractors on contracts valued up to $1,000,000. The contracts may be for construction, supplies, or services provided by either a prime or subcontractor.

In 1990, 9,900 contractors were helped. The loan guarantees for 1992 are expected to be over $1,500,000,000 dollars.

Contact: Office of Surety Guarantees, Small Business Administration, 4040 N. Fairfax Dr., Arlington, VA 22203. Phone Howard Huegel at (703) 235-2900.

Local Development Company Loans

Groups of local citizens whose aim is to improve the economy in their area can get a **Certified Development Company Loan.** Loan proceeds may be used to finance residential or commercial construction or rehabilitation of property for sale.

In 1990, 1,555 loans were made. The estimated total money available for 1992 is $506,000,000.

Contact: Office of Economic Development, Small Business Administration, Room 720, 409 3rd Street SW, Washington, DC 20416. Phone (202) 653-6416.

Start a Small Airline

If you'd like to provide air services to small towns, the Department of Transportation may be able to help. They subsidize service to approximately 150 communities that would not otherwise have air access. The payments cover costs and return needs. The annual payments range from $90,000 to $400,000 per destination. Approximately $28,000,000 was paid in 1988.

Contact: Director, Office of Aviation Analysis, P-50, Department of Transportation, 400 Seventh Street SW, Washington, DC 20590. Phone (202) 366-5903.

Flood Insurance

The Federal Insurance Administration enables persons and small businesses to purchase insurance against losses from physical damage to buildings and their contents. The premium rate is generally lower than a normal actuarial rate, reflecting a subsidy by the Federal Government. Maximum coverage is $250,000 for small business structures and $300,000 for the contents.

The FIA has a large number of booklets available, which explains the program, design guidelines for floor damage reduction, how to understand flood insurance rate maps, etc.

Contact: Federal Insurance Administration, FEMA, Washington, DC 20472. Phone Amy Coxson at (202) 646-2774.

Wrestling with Tax Matters

The *Your Business Tax Kit,* was developed for presentation to operators of new businesses as they are formed. Its purpose is to encourage more effective voluntary compliance by helping new business persons become fully aware of their responsibilities for filing all the Federal tax returns for which they may be liable and for paying the taxes due.

The kit is an envelope designed to hold forms and instructions for preparing most business tax returns.

Kits may either be picked up at an IRS office or will be mailed to the taxpayer upon request.

Small Business Tax Workshops are conducted regularly throughout the country. For more information or to request a publication, call toll-free (800) 829-1040.

Emergency Loans for Farmers and Ranchers

The **Farmers Home Administration** has loans to assist family farmers, ranchers and agriculture operators to cover losses suffered from major disasters. Loans may be used to repair, restore, or replace damaged property and supplies and, under some circumstances, to refinance debts.

The maximum loan is $500,000; the interest rate is 4.5 percent. In 1990, 2,607 loans totaling $73,000,000 were made.

Contact: Farmers Home Administration, Department of Agriculture, Washington, DC 20250. Phone (202) 382-1632.

Loans for Non-Profit Corporations

The **Farmers Home Administration** has loans, loan guarantees, and grants to rural development and finance corporations that improve business, industry and employment in rural areas through the stimulation of private investment and foundation contributions.

The non-profit corporation may serve profit or nonprofit businesses but they must be local. The corporation must be authorized to do business in at least three states.

For more information, contact: Administrator, Farmers Home Administration, Department of Agriculture, Washington, DC 20250. Phone (202) 447-7967.

Money for *Not* Growing Stuff

If your green thumb has turned yellow, this is for you. For
not growing crops such as cotton, corn, sorghum, barley,
oats, wheat, or rice, the Department of Agriculture will
reward you. What's the catch? You must do this by reducing
the amount you usually produce.

Contact: Commodity Analysis Division, Agricultural
Stabilization and Conservation Service, P.O. Box 2415, U.S.
Department of Agriculture, Washington, DC 20013. Phone
(202) 447-7641 or 447-5074.

Small Forest Projects

If you own 1,000 acres or less of forest land capable of
producing industrial wood crops, the Forestry Incentives
Program may be of interest to you. The government will
share up to 65% of the cost of tree planting, timber stand
improvement, and site preparation. In 1992 approximately
$12,000,000 in cost-share assistance will be provided.

Contact: Conservation and Environmental Protection
Division, Department of Agriculture, P.O. Box 2415,
Washington, DC 20013. Phone (202) 447-6221.

Money for Ships

The Department of Transportation Maritime Administration
will provide loan guarantees to promote the construction of
ships for foreign and domestic commerce.

The vessels must be designed for research or for commercial
use in coastal or intercoastal trade, on the Great Lakes, on
bays, rivers, and lakes of the U.S., in foreign trade, or as
floating drydocks. Any ship not less than five net tons (other
than a towboat, barge, scow, lighter, canal boat or tank vessel
of less than 25 gross tons) is eligible.

The ship owner must provide 25% of the total cost. These
guarantees have been used to build large ships such as
tankers, ocean-going liners, dredges, jack-up drilling rigs,

and container ships. Numerous smaller ships including ocean-going and inland tugs and barges have also been funded.

Contact: Associate Administrator for Maritime Aids, Maritime Administration, Department of Transportation, Washington, DC 20590. Phone (202) 366-0364.

Mortgage Insurance

If you rent housing to low or middle income, the elderly, in urban renewal areas, or are a credit risk because of low income, the Department of Housing and Urban Development may be able to help by providing mortgage insurance.

Contact: Insurance Division, Office of Insured Multifamily Housing Development, Department of Housing and Urban Development, Washington, DC 20410. Phone (202) 755-6223.

Grants for Designing People

Grants for architecture, landscaping, fashion design, interior decorating, and urban design are available from the National Endowment of the Arts.

Examples of projects that have been funded are: an urban design plan for the revitalization of a city waterfront district, a design competition for a museum of fine arts, adaptive reuse of unused school buildings, and the potential uses for vacant and derelict land in American cities.

In 1992 over $3,000,000 will be awarded. Ask for the booklets *National Endowment for the Arts, Guide to Programs* and *Design Arts Guidelines*.

Contact: Director, Design Arts Program, National Endowment for the Arts, 1100 Pennsylvania Avenue NW, Washington, DC 20506. Phone (202) 682-5437.

Grants, Grants, and More Grants

The following are examples of grants being given by the Federal government. Since these come and go it is essential to check for up-to-date information with each department.

National Endowment for the Arts
1100 Pennsylvania Avenue NW
Washington, DC 20506

> Document Preservation
> Dance Companies
> Film/Video of Art of Dance
> Art Services
> Experimental Initiatives
> Traditional Art
> Folk Art
> Innovative Art
> Writers and Translators
> Literary Distribution
> Literary Magazines
> Small Press Assistance
> Residencies for Writers
> Audience Development
> Narrative Film Development
> Radio Production
> Radio Workshops
> Museum Services
> Museum Projects
> Music Presentations
> Music Festivals
> Jazz Projects
> Music Ensembles
> Choruses
> Composers
> Creative Orchestra
> Solo Recitalists

  Music Recording
  Theater Works
  Regional Touring
  Mime
  Producers
  Theater Training
  Playwrights
  Visual Artists
  Art Education
  Translations
  Humanities
  Preservation of Newspapers

Emergency Management Agency
Washington, DC 20472
Telephone (202) 646-3363
    Emergency Broadcast Systems

Department of Justice
National Institute of Corrections
320 First Street Room 200
Washington, DC 20534
Telephone (202) 724-3106
    Improvement of corrections programs
    Research of criminal behavior
    Training of corrections staff
    Juvenile crime research

Bureau of Land Management
Department of Interior
Washington, DC 20240
Telephone (202) 653-9200
    Management of public lands

Community Planning and Development
Office of Urban Rehabilitation
451 7th Street SW
Washington, DC 20410

Telephone (202) 755-6996
    Neighborhood rehabilitation

Department of Energy
Forrestal Building
Room 5B-110
Washington, DC 20585
Telephone (202) 586-1593
        Energy research
        Fossil energy
        Nuclear energy
        Renewable energy
        Coal technology
        Basic energy research

Economic Development Administration
Department of Commerce
Room H-7317
Washington, DC 20230
Telephone (202) 377-4085
        Chronic economic depression
        Economic development

Office of Vocational and Adult Education
Department of Education
400 Maryland Avenue SW Room 519
Washington, DC 20202
Telephone (202) 732-2362
        Adult Education
        Bilingual Instruction
        Foreign Language Studies
        Indian and Hawaiian Native Education

Department of Health and Human Services
Washington, DC 20201
        Dentistry
        Developmental disabilities
        Nursing research

Nursing training
Population research
Aging research
International biomedical exchanges
Mental health research
Alcohol abuse
Biophysics and Physiological Sciences
Clinical research
Retinal and choroidal research
Anterior segment research
Microbiology and Infectious Diseases research
Immunology
Kidney Disease
Diabetes research
Lung research
Heart research
Arthritis research
Cancer research
AIDS research
Animal research

Environmental Protection Agency
Grants Administration Division
PM 216
Washington, DC 20460
Telephone (202) 382-7473
Solid waste disposal
Hazardous waste disposal
Air pollution research
Pesticides control

Department of Interior
Geological Survey
MS 424
National Center
Reston, VA 22092
Telephone (703) 648-6810
Water resources research

National Oceanic and Atmospheric Administration
6010 Executive Blvd
Rockville, MD 20852
Telephone (301) 443-8415
> Climate and atmospheric research
> Marine research

Soil Conservation Office
Department of Agriculture
P.O. Box 2890
Washington, DC 20250
Telephone (202) 447-4527
> Abandoned Mine Program
> Agricultural research

National Science Foundation
1800 C Street NW
Washington, DC 20550
> Scientific, Technological and International Affairs
> Biological, Behavioral, and Social Sciences
> Geosciences
> Mathematical and Physical Sciences
> Engineering research

Some Money-Raising Hints to Get to Uncle Sam & Others

The Small Business Administration (SBA) is always first in mind for Uncle Sugar handouts. It ain't necessarily so. True, billions of dollars have been dispensed by this agency, but equally true that much of this was never repaid and getting new business bucks today is not always easy.

The SBA will consider a loan or loan guaranty only if two commercial banking sources have turned you down. however, while a bank might lend you money for 5 to 7 years, the SBA can help extend the loan over 10 years–thus spreading out the payback and helping your cash flow.

The SBA is more favorably inclined toward minorities.

The SBA will lend money in distressed areas, while most banks will not.

The SBA may lend money with a lower credit rating than a bank would, although the SBA will probably insist on personal guaranties such as collateral on your home), while a bank might be satisfied with only commercial guaranties.

The SBA is not the only government source of loans. The Federal government has about a thousand different loan programs through virtually all of its departments. Ask the SBA.

If you buy a business, you might have to pay "key money"; have this subjective portion of the purchase price included in the total (paying the seller only $1 for good will or a non-compete clause) and get a loan on the total amount—in this way you can probably borrow 100% of the purchase price and save your own cash for operating the business.

Remember that seller-financing beats SBA or bank financing.

Remember also the cynic's advice—that the best number to know is the telephone number of a rich relative.

When making any kind of loan, remember the three Cs and prepare them carefully in advance of your application: **credit, cash flow, collateral**. if you cannot satisfactorily answer the three-C requirements, keep your job.

Don't overlook your own and your immediate family's fiscal resources. These might surprise you. The more you can gather together from all resources, the less you need to borrow and the less you need to pay back. It also makes your personal statement look better and easier to get more money from the SBA or banks. Financial people know that if you are willing to share in the risk, they are less likely to say 'no.'

What to Do if the Government Won't Give You a Loan

A different approach to owning a successful business avoids loans from institutions. A brief outline of the technique goes as follows:

- **Many new businesses fail,** so avoid this obstacle by buying a proven successful business.

- **All businesses are for sale.** The next time you go into a business that looks prosperous and interesting to you, ask who the owner is. If he's on the premises, go into his office; if not, phone him from the nearest phone booth. Ask him, "Have you ever thought about selling this business?" The answer is always yes. Tell him you're interested. Plan on seeing him a number of times for informal discussions.

- **The owner will ask you, "How much have you got to put down?"** Say that the amount put down depends on the financial status of the company, but you will need some owner financing. Usually he or she will say that if you will put 20 to 30% down, they'll provide financing. Be sure to ask for twenty- to thirty-year financing. *Don't worry about not having the down payment in hand.*

- **Make sure the company makes a good profit;** it is easier to buy a company that has $200,000 to $300,000 a year profit than it is to buy one that makes $10,000 a year profit. Besides going through the books, ask their suppliers. Suppliers know which businesses are profitable.

- **Is the company run by a manager?** Has he been there more than five years? If so, ask him if he'll stay if you buy the business.

● **Who are the suppliers?** Contact them and ask them what they think about the prospective business. If they are enthused, tell them you want to buy the business and will need some "working capital" *(this is your down payment but never call it that).* You may need to grant concessions such as the exclusive rights to supply you. There is a large variety of interbusiness financial agreements. Usually one will fit your purposes. *This is the largest source of business loans in the U.S. today.*

That's the approach in a nutshell. There are many variations on the theme.

There are a number of seminars that teach this basic method. Watch for one in your area.

Chapter 8

International Trade

Trade Information Center

The **Trade Promotion Coordinating Committee** (TPCC) has been established in the Department of Commerce as the "one-stop-shop" for information on U.S. Government programs and activities that support your exporting efforts.

For information on:

- Export Counseling

- Seminars and Conferences

- Overseas Buyers and Representatives

- Overseas Events

- Export Financing

- Technical Assistance

Contact: Trade Information Center, Department of
Commerce, Washington, DC 20230, Phone (800) 872-8723.
FAX (202) 377-4473. TDD (800) 833-8723.

Export Counseling and Financial Assistance

The **Office of International Trade** facilitates financial
assistance and other appropriate management and technical
assistance to small business concerns that have the potential
to become successful exporters. The program provides basic
export counseling and training which includes:

- one-on-one counseling by SCORE/ACE volunteers
  with significant international trade expertise

- access to university research and counseling

- assistance from professional international trade
  management consulting firms

- referral to other public or private sector expertise

- initial consultation with an international trade attorney
  of the Federal Bar Association

- business management training

- international trade and export marketing publications.

Contact: Office of International Trade, Small Business
Administration, 409 3rd Street SW, 6th Floor, Washington,
DC 20416. Phone (202) 205-7527.

Export Seminars

The **Bureau of Export Administration's** seminar staff
teaches exporters about the national security requirements for
international sales. U.S. exporters and foreign importers of
American products around the world increase their
knowledge and understanding of U.S. Export Regulations by
attending classroom instruction offered by the export seminar

staff. The Export Administration Regulations Course is a professional seminar featuring two or three days of classroom training on export controls and licensing procedures.

Seminars are held in major cities throughout the United States and in foreign countries. Both introductory and advanced courses on the Export Administration Regulations are offered. Completing the introductory course is a prerequisite for receiving advanced instruction.

The seminars assist a business in understanding the requirements for compliance with U.S. export laws and procedures, to improve its ability to use and understand Federal export regulations, to prepare better license applications and other documentation, to find out how a company can avoid the costly fines and time-consuming seizures that result from violation of export laws, and to discover ways to increase productivity, ease license application efforts, and lower costs of doing business abroad.

These seminars have proven valuable to manufacturers, carriers, shipping agents, freight forwarders, international sales and marketing specialists, contracts administrators, materials and traffic managers, customer service representatives, buyers, accountants, attorneys, freight forwarders, technical supervisors, order processors, and export licensing coordinators.

Contact: Bureau of Export Administration, Department of Commerce, 14th & Constitution Avenue NW, HCHB Room 1099D, Washington, DC 20230. Phone (202) 377-8731.

Export Management and Marketing Help for Smaller Businesses

The Agency for International Development (AID), implements the U.S. Foreign Economic Assistance Program in more than 80 countries throughout Africa, Europe, Near East, Asia, Latin America and the Caribbean. OSDBU offers counseling services and marketing assistance to U.S. firms interested in exporting goods, and technical assistance through AID-financed projects.

AID participates in two set-aside programs: the SBA 8(a) program, and the Small Business Set-aside program. Unique to AID is the Gray Amendment which requires that 10% of prime contracts be setaside for socially and economically disadvantaged businesses, women-owned businesses, historically Black Colleges and Universities, U.S. colleges and universities with at least 40% enrollment of Hispanic American students, and minority-controlled private voluntary organizations.

The Office maintains the AID Consultant Registry Information System (ACRIS), an automated database identifying U.S. businesses and their area of expertise.

As legislatively mandated and for the benefit of U.S. businesses, AID publishes, free of charge, Procurement Information Bulletins advertising intended procurement of AID financed commodities (goods, products, material). To subscribe to the Bulletins, request a mailing list application from OSDBU.

These notices are available free of charge by completing a mailing list application available from the office.

Contact: Agency for International Development, Room 1400-A, SA-14, Washington, DC 20523-1414. Phone (703) 875-1551.

Overseas Promotion of Your Product

The International Trade Administration's **Export Promotion Services** will assist exporters through a variety of programs and services that analyze foreign markets, locate buyers and representatives overseas, and promote products and services. In addition, they offer export counseling services for all aspects of the export process. International trade experts are located worldwide in 66 U.S. cities and 127 overseas cities.

Trade Fairs are shop windows in which thousands of firms from many countries display their wares. These fairs are international marketplaces in which buyers and sellers can meet conveniently.

A **Trade Fair Certification Program** advises and assists sponsors of these fairs in promoting the events; gives the fairs official Department of Commerce recognition, and counsels exhibitors. In addition, official U.S. participation is sponsored in key international trade fairs in all parts of the world.

Three types of trade missions have been developed to help U.S. exporters penetrate overseas markets. **Specialized Trade Missions** bring groups of U.S. business people into direct contact with potential foreign buyers, agents, and distributors.

Seminar Missions promote sales of sophisticated products and technology in markets where sales can be achieved more effectively by presenting technical seminars or concentrating on concepts and systems. They feature one- and two-day presentations by a team of U.S. industry representatives who conduct discussions on the technology of their industry.

Industry-Organized Government-Approved (IOGA) Trade Missions are organized by trade associations, chambers of commerce, state development agencies, and similar groups with the advice and support of the agency.

In addition to product exhibitions, the overseas Export Development Office facilities are available to trade associations and to individual firms or their agents for Business-Sponsored Promotions (BSPs). BSPs may include sales meetings, conferences, or seminars. Finally, Catalog Exhibitions and Video/Catalog Exhibitions are low-cost, flexible kinds of exhibitions that can provide U.S. industry with an effective technique to give products exposure overseas, test the salability of the products, develop sales leads, and identify potential buyers, agents, or distributors.

Both are held at U.S. Embassies or Consulates or in conjunction with trade shows. These two kinds of exhibitions are especially useful in promoting U.S. exports in remote and small markets of the world where major equipment exhibitions are not feasible.

Contact: International Trade Administration, United States and Foreign Commercial Service, Department of Commerce, Export Promotion Services, 14th & Constitution Avenue NW, Room 2116H, Washington, DC 20230. Phone (202) 377-4231.

Applying for an Export License

The **Bureau of Export Administration** has several services to assist in the licensing process. This office is the bureau's licensing 'customer service unit' staffed with licensing information experts. It helps solve or answer most exporters' questions about 'How to apply for an export license.' By telephone or mail, these experts can help you prepare license applications and guide you through export regulations.

In developing an export strategy, companies need to review the U.S. export laws as they relate to a planned export. For reasons of national security, export of certain technologies is controlled through two types of export licenses: general and validated.

This office should be called when you have a specific question about export regulations or current policy, need license information on overseas trade fairs, have an emergency license request that may need special handling, or want to find out your licensing case number.

ELAIN (Electronic License Application Information Network) allows on-line computer acceptance of export license applications for all free world destinations. ELAIN offers U.S. exporters a fast and convenient way to submit or receive license applications. After receiving applications, the office processes, reviews, and issues the license electronically. Applications may cover all commodities except super-computers.

First, exporters apply for authorization to submit applications electronically by writing to the address above to the attention of ELAIN. The exporter should provide the name and address of the applicant company, a phone number, and the name of the contact person.

The **Office of Exporting Licensing** will provide information on how to obtain company identifications numbers and personal identification numbers to individuals approved by the office and the exporting company to submit license applications. The exporter will also receive instructions on how to contact the CompuServe computer network to obtain detailed filing instructions.

Once exporters have the necessary authorization to begin submitting license applications electronically to ELAIN, they will be able to enter license related information into their own personal computers and send it over telephone lines via CompuServe to the Commerce Department. Licensing decisions will be electronically conveyed back to exporters, again via the CompuServe network.

They'll help you get export licensing publications and forms, the most important of which is *Export Administration Regulations.*

Since the Bureau of Export Administration receives between 500 and 600 applications every working day, it is important for a business to obtain these information publications early in the marketing stage so that it fully understands the export licensing program.

To subscribe to the ***Export Administration Regulations*** contact the Superintendent of Documents, U.S. GPO, Washington, DC 20402. Phone (202) 783-3238. Reference subscription number 903-012-00000-5.

Exporters may obtain forms required by the bureau by calling the Exporter Assistance staff at (202) 377-8731 or writing Bureau of Export Administration, Department of Commerce, P.O. Box 273, Washington, DC 20044. ATTN: FORMS.

STELA (System for Tracking Export License Applications) is a computer-generated voice unit that interfaces with the Department of Commerce ECASS (Export Control Automated Support System) database. It provides accurate and timely information on the status of license applications.

STELA tells an exporter exactly where an application is in the system and for how long it has been there. It can also give an exporter authority to ship his or her goods for those applications approved without conditions. Exporters still receive a hard copy of the license by mail, but an exporter can ship with STELA's approval before receiving it.

Exporters, with a touch-tone phone, can call STELA at (202) 377-2752, it will answer "Hello, I'm STELA, the Department of Commerce export license system. Please enter your license application number or hang up." Using the pushbuttons on the phone, enter the license application number. Following the entry, in synthesized voice response, STELA gives the status of the case. If you need to talk to a person about STELA, call (202) 377-2572.

STELA can also handle questions about the amendment applications. After announcing the status of one case, STELA prompts the caller to enter another case number or hang up. STELA is in operation weekdays from 7:15 a.m. to 11:15 p.m. EST and on Saturdays from 8:00 a.m. to 4:00 p.m. The database is updated each night, so an application's status should be checked only once a day.

Contact: Bureau of Export Administration, Department of Commerce, 14th & Constitution Avenue NW, HCHB Room 1099D, Washington, DC 20230. Phone (202) 377-4811 in Washington, DC or (714) 660-0144 in Newport Beach, CA.

How To Find New Opportunities in Foreign Markets

Competition in the world market is becoming ever more challenging and foreign governments have increased support for their exporters. The Export Trading Company Act of 1982 offers U.S. business new opportunities to compete in foreign markets. The goal of this legislation is to encourage the development of American Export Trading Companies (ETC), particularly for the benefit of small and medium-sized companies.

This office promotes and encourages the formation of ETCs, counsels firms interested in exporting, provides a contact facilitation service between U.S. producers and firms providing export trade services, administers the Title III Antitrust Certificate of Review Program, and conducts ETC conferences.

Contact: The Export Trading Company Affairs Office, International Trade Administration, Trade Development, Department of Commerce, 14th & Constitution Avenue NW, Washington, DC 20230. Phone (202) 377-5131.

Identifying and Evaluating Overseas Markets

The new **Commercial Information Management System (CIMS)** electronically links all the economic and marketing information of ITA trade specialists and offices worldwide, allowing vital business data to be delivered on a timely basis.

Custom tailored market research information packages are available on;

- foreign business and economic climate

- import regulations

- tariff and non-tariff barriers

- domestic and foreign competition

- individual competitor firms and competitive factors

- distribution practices

- how products are promoted in the market

- policies

- product standards

- end users.

In addition, CIMS can provide information on; foreign agents, distributors, importers, manufacturers, retailers, government purchasing officials, and end users interested in your product or service type. CIMS can provide tailored to your specifications;

- names of contacts

- telex FAX, cable, and phone numbers

- product or service specialties

- year established

- number of employees

- relative size of firms

Contact: CIMS Market Research, International Trade Administration, United States and Foreign Commercial Service, Department of Commerce, 14th & Constitution Avenue NW, Washington, DC 20230.

Lists of Overseas Customers and Companies

The Export Information Systems (XIS) **Data Reports** provides lists of the largest markets and competition sources for a company's products.

XIS is an export/import data bank of trade information of approximately 2,500 product categories showing their performance in the world market. This information is based on Standard International Trade Classification (SITC) statistics supplied by the United Nations. XIS produces two kinds of reports:

- Product Reports give information on the top 35 import markets for a product and on the top 25 world markets for U.S. exporters, based on the percentage of market share and dollar sales volume.

- Country Reports give information on the top 20 products imported into a specific country, the top 10 U.S. products imported into the country, by market share and the top 10 U.S. products imported into the country, by sales volume.

Contact: Export Information Systems (XIS), Small Business Administration, Office of International Trade, 409 3rd Street SW—6th Floor, Washington, DC 20146.

Advertising to 100,000 Foreign Executives, Distributors, and Government Officials

Commercial News USA promotes U.S. products and services available for export to more than 100,000 overseas agents, distributors, government officials, and end-users. Additional distribution is made of selected products and services through reprints in local media.

Commercial News USA contains descriptions of 150 to 200 products, services, and trade and technical literature with black and white photographs in each issue. In addition to featuring general new products, all issues highlight individual industries and receive special promotion by U.S. commercial officers overseas at industry trade events.

While much depends on the product being promoted, firms typically average thirty to forty inquiries each and initial sales averaging over $10,000. There is a fee for advertising in the magazine.

Contact: International Trade Administration, United States and Foreign Commercial Service, Department of Commerce, 14th & Constitution Avenue NW, Washington, DC 20230. Phone (202) 377-4918.

Trade Leads on Overseas Sales
Opportunities for Agricultural-Related Products

The **AgExport Connections Trade Lead Service** provides continual access to timely sales leads from overseas firms seeking to buy or represent American food and agricultural products. Businesses have a direct pipeline to trade leads gathered by Foreign Agricultural Service (FAS) offices worldwide.

Both new and established American exporters can use trade leads as a fundamental sales tool which brings foreign buyers' purchasing needs directly to them.

Each day, FAS agricultural counselors, attachés, and trade officers around the world locate and develop trade opportunities. They find sales opportunities with foreign companies, government purchasing agencies, brokers, distributors and others, and determine information needed to pursue each trade lead-product specifications such as labeling and packaging, quantities, end uses, delivery deadlines, bid requirements, telex/cable contact points, and mailing addresses. These trade leads are then forwarded to AgExport within hours, and distributed.

Leads are available the same day to U.S. exporters through a number of commercial computerized information networks. Trade leads also can be mailed daily to clients in the United States who have subscribed to a special mail service.

A bulletin is available which includes ALL trade leads processed each week. It is mailed weekly and is targeted toward export agents, trade associations, and companies interested in export opportunities for a wide variety of food and agricultural products.

The bulletin also highlights upcoming trade shows, foreign trade developments, and changes and updates in trade policy. Specialists can also generate various mailing lists of prospective buyers for you.

Contact: Foreign Agricultural Service, Department of
Agriculture, AgExport, 14th & Independence Avenue SW,
Room 4639-S, Washington, DC 20250. Phone
(202) 447-7103.

Help for Food Exporters

The **Label Clearance Program** (LCP) was designed to help
U.S. food processors and exporters locate foreign markets
and sales opportunities for U.S. commodities new to overseas
markets.

Although many of these products have long since been tested
and accepted by American customers, the products have not
been marketed in many foreign countries.

Each participating U.S. firm is provided with information on
the foreign countries' requirements for imported foods.
Without this information the job of exporting to a foreign
market can be costly and time-consuming.

The LCP review can answer such questions as: where must
the country of origin appear on the label; in what order must
the product ingredients be listed; what is the required
language and are bilingual labels or stick-ons acceptable, *et
al.*

The LCP office conducts a screening of each company's
label and product information to ensure completeness before
it is submitted for overseas evaluation. Once this screening is
completed the information is forwarded to LCP review in the
targeted country.

The final product specific report prepared by an overseas
post contains a brief statement on the product's marketability
in the specific overseas country. This objective assessment of
the product's ability to compete in the targeted market is
provided to assist the U.S. firm in its evaluation of the
product's competitiveness.

A new part of the LCP Services is the Country Product
Clearance Summary. This report provides the participating

company with a concise statement on the taste and eating
habits of the country, information on the legal requirements
and standards that govern the packaging and labeling of
imported foods, and the business customs of the targeted
country.

Summary reports for Japan, Mexico, Germany, Switzerland,
and France have been completed.

Contact: The Label Clearance Program, Foreign Agricultural
Service, Department of Agriculture, High Value Products
Division, 14th & Independence Avenue SW, Room 4649-S,
Washington, DC 20250. Phone (202) 447-7103.

Advertising Your Agricultural Products Overseas

A monthly newsletter, *Contacts for U.S. Agricultural
Products*, assists American firms by introducing their food
and agricultural products to foreign markets. It is sent to
Foreign Agricultural Service counselors, attachés, and trade
officers for distribution to prospective foreign buyers.

It is translated into Japanese, Spanish, French, Italian and
Greek and mailed to thousands of buyers worldwide. Brief,
100-word descriptions of products submitted by U.S. firms
are published each month.

Contact: Foreign Agricultural Service, Department of
Agriculture, Agricultural Information and Marketing Service,
14th & Independence Avenue SW, Room 4649-S,
Washington, DC 20250. Phone (202) 447-7103.

When an Export Licensing Emergency Occurs

A business may have an emergency requiring immediate
attention. In justifiable emergencies, generally when the
situation is out of the applicant's control, the applicant or his
authorized agent should contact this office or the nearest
district office to expedite handling of an application.

The validity of a license issued under this special processing
procedure expires no later than the last day of the month

following the month of issuance. Because a company is expected to use a license issued on an emergency basis immediately, the office of Export Licensing will not extend the validity period of a license.

Contact: Bureau of Export Administration, Office of Export Licensing, Department of Commerce, 14th & Pennsylvania Avenue NW, HCHB Room 1099D, Washington, DC 20230. Phone (202) 377-4811 (Washington, DC) or (714) 660-0144 (Newport Beach, CA).

When You Need Technical Answers for Products Under Export Control

At the request of exporters, advisory options and classification determinations are issued on commodities to be exported from the United States.

The **Technology and Policy Analysis Office** is responsible for establishing export control policy under the authority of the Export Administration Act.

It develops, in association with other U.S. agencies and the International Coordinating Committee (COCOM), export control and decontrol proposals. It analyzes and develops national security, foreign policy, and short supply control programs; revises and develops implementing Export Administration Regulations, and reviews and resolves technical and policy issues related to export applications and appeals of licensing determinations.

Contact: Technology and Policy Analysis Office, Bureau of Export Administration, Department of Commerce, 14th & Constitution Avenue NW, HCHB Room 4069A, Washington, DC 20230. Phone (202) 377-4188.

Referrals for Export Related Data Processing Services

This new service is offered to businesses and others who want to file export documents electronically but do not have access to needed computer hardware and/or software.

The bureau will provide a brochure listing service agencies that have registered with the **Census Bureau** and that can provide one or more of these services: develop or provide computer software, edit raw data; transmit electronic data to the bureau; provide data on computer tape or floppy diskettes, or provide current listings of all commodity classifications.

Registered organizations can supply the services for which they are listed.

Contact: National Clearinghouse for Export Data Processing Services, Bureau of the Census, Automated Reporting Branch, Department of Commerce, Foreign Trade Division, Room 2176, Washington, DC 20233. Phone (301) 763-7774.

Locating Overseas Representatives for Your Firm

A unique program provides custom overseas searches for interested and qualified foreign representatives on behalf of a U.S. client.

U.S. commercial officers abroad conduct the search on a single country and prepare a report identifying up to six foreign prospects that have personally examined the U.S. firm's product literature and have expressed interest in representing the firm.

Contact: Agent/Distributor Service (ADS), International Trade Administration, United States and Foreign Commercial Service, Department of Commerce, Washington, DC 20230. Phone (202) 377-2432.

Opportunities in Latin America and the Caribbean.

The U.S. Department of Commerce is the U.S. Government agency responsible for promoting U.S. exports and strengthening the United States' position in international trade. To support the Caribbean Basin Initiative and the Enterprise for the Americas Initiative, the Department established the Latin America/Caribbean Business

Development Center (LACBDC), with a mandate to assist U.S. companies to take advantage of trade and investment opportunities arising from these programs. A separate office, the Caribbean Basin Division, monitors economic conditions and commercial policy issues and provides business counselling to U.S. exporters. The Division is a particularly useful asset to new-to-market or infrequent exporters.

Latin America/Caribbean Business Development Center

The Department of Commerce, in cooperation with the Agency for International Development (AID), established the LACBDC to support the U.S. Government commitment to regional economic prosperity through greater private sector activity. The LACBDC is designed to assist both U.S. and Latin American/Caribbean firms to take advantage of opportunities arising from the Caribbean Basin Initiative and the Enterprise for the Americas Initiative. For more information contact:

> Latin America/Caribbean Business Development Center
> Room H-3203
> U.S. Department of Commerce
> Washington, DC 20230
> Telephone: (202) 377-0703
> FAX: (202) 377-2218

Companies located in the Caribbean and Central America can take advantage of the close working relationship between the Department of Commerce and AID by contacting the AID private sector officer(s) and the senior commercial officer at the U.S. embassy. Caribbean Basin companies can also contact the LACBDC directly and can list private trade and investment opportunities in the Center's monthly *Business Bulletin*.

U.S. firms are also urged to contact the Department of Commerce's District Offices located throughout the United States for useful trade and investment information. For the location of the nearest District Office, look under the "U.S. Government" section of the local telephone directory.

LA/C Center Programs to assist Caribbean Basin companies with the process of exporting products to the United States or promoting investment include the following:

- **U.S. Regional Seminars:** These seminars will be held throughout the United States to inform the U.S. private sector on trade and investment opportunities.

- **Business Development Missions:** Missions to the region and reverse missions to the United States will be organized to assist Caribbean Basin companies in doing business with the United States and in locating U.S. buyers and investors.

- **LA/C Business Bulletin:** This monthly publication will supplant the previously published *CBI Business Bulletin*. Former *CBI Business Bulletin* subscribers will automatically receive the new publication. Caribbean Basin companies are encouraged to list their company and available trade and/or investment opportunities in the Bulletin.

- **Business Counseling:** LA/C Center specialists will help Caribbean Basin companies identify markets and find programs tailored to their needs.

- **Infrastructure/Sectoral Projects:** The Center develops long-term projects addressing obstacles to CBI implementation. Examples include investor attitude studies and country-by-country assessments of the business-related telecommunication and energy sectors. These and other projects enhance the business climate by improving the infrastructure and general business environment.

Caribbean Basin Division

Apart from promoting U.S. exports to the Caribbean Basin, the Caribbean Basin Division focuses on specific issues and problems of doing business in the region. In conjunction with their primary role of supporting U.S. export programs, the CBD focuses on policy-related issues between the United States and Caribbean and Central American countries. For more information contact: Caribbean Basin Division, Room 3025, International Trade Administration, International Economic Policy, Department of Commerce, 14th & Constitution Avenue NW, Washington, DC 20230. Phone (202) 377-2527.

Eastern Europe Business Information Center

The Center is stocked with a wide range of publications on doing business in Eastern Europe; these include lists of potential partners, investment regulations, priority industry sectors, and notices of upcoming seminars, conferences and trade promotion events. It also serves as a referral point for programs of voluntary assistance to the region.

Contact: Eastern Europe Business Information Center, (202) 377-2645, FAX (202) 377-4473.

Gulf Reconstruction Center

The Gulf Reconstruction Center coordinates the Department of Commerce's reconstruction activities and counsels the U.S. business community about rebuilding opportunities in Kuwait and the Gulf region. The Center serves as an information clearinghouse for business visitors. It also provides American firms with materials on doing business in Kuwait. The center is compiling a database of companies interested in business opportunities in the region, which can also be used by the Kuwaiti Government and the U.S. Army

Corps of Engineers to obtain information on companies interested in Kuwait's reconstruction effort.

Contact: Counseling and Referral Services, Gulf Reconstruction Center, (202) 377-5767, FAX (202) 377-0878.

To Reach an Export Specialist for a Specific Country

Where should a U.S. exporter go to find out about agent/distributor agreements in Saudi Arabia? About how to recover a business debt resulting from Mexico's foreign exchange crisis? About Canada's investment approval process? About a trade show in Germany? About countertrade with Tanzania? About tariff rates in Paraguay?

The best sources of information on such matters are **country desk officers** who can handle such questions and provide other useful commercial information as well.

These specialists perform a unique service. They look at the needs of the individual U.S. firm wishing to sell in a particular country in the full context of that country's overall economy, trade policies and political situation, and also in the light of U.S. policies toward the country.

Desk officers keep up to date on the economic and commercial conditions in their assigned countries. Each collects information on the country's regulations, tariffs, business practices, economic and political developments including trade data and trends, market size and growth that affect ability to do business. Each keeps tabs on the country's potential as a market for U.S. products and services and for U.S. investment.

Call (202) 377-2000 and ask for the export specialist for the country you're interested in, or see Appendix 3.

To write them: Country Export Specialists, International Trade Administration, International Economic Policy, Department of Commerce, 14th & Constitution Avenue NW, Room 3864, Washington, DC 20230.

Export Management and Networking Assistance Near You

Businesses help promote and assist in increasing U.S. exports through the International Trade Administration's **District Export Councils**. The councils work to enlist the efforts of the American business community to help government expand export opportunities and increase U.S. exports abroad.

There are 51 councils with 1800 members representing every state and territory of the United States. They have an increased role in the development of U.S. trade policy. Organized work plans are developed by each council to carry out initiatives locally to promote exporting.

The councils have become a vital multiplier in export awareness and promotion and represent a local voice in the establishment of trade policies. Firms interested in contacting their local councils should call this office.

Contact: District Export Councils, International Trade Administration, United States and Foreign Commercial Service, Department of Commerce, 14th & Constitution Avenue NW, Washington, DC 20230. Phone (202) 377-4767.

Where To Get Trade Data, Competitive Assessments, and Analysis Data

The **Trade Information and Analysis Program** monitors and provides trade data, conducts macro-economic trade research and analysis, assesses U.S. industrial competitiveness, and operates an Office of Trade Finance, which offers counseling on offset/countertrade practices to U.S. exporters.

The program also produces a series of publications, such as *Industrial Outlook, Competitive Assessments, Trade Performance,* and *U.S. Foreign Trade Highlights*.

Industrial Outlook, published annually, features assessments and forecasts of business conditions for more than 350 industries. It is available at any Government Printing Office for $24.

Competitive Assessments are periodic reports which assess the medium- and long-range competitiveness of specific U.S. industries in international trade.

Some recent titles include **Cement, Automobile, Materials Handling Equipment, Sporting Goods, Cellular Radio Equipment, International Construction, Computer Systems, Civil Helicopters**, and **Fiber Optics**. These are available at any Government Printing Office at a cost of between $3 and $7.

The Trade Performance series, published annually, provides a detailed analytical look at the U.S. trade performance and positions.

The *U.S. Foreign Trade Highlights*, published annually, details trade data trends in U.S. foreign trade in selected regions and with major trading partners. The current issue is available at any Government Printing Office.

Contact a Government Printing Office or International Trade Administration, Trade Development, Department of Commerce, 14th & Constitution Avenue NW, Washington, DC 20230. Phone (202) 377-1316.

Sales Leads from Overseas Firms

The **Trade Opportunities Program** (TOP) provides timely sales leads, joint ventures, and licensing opportunities from overseas firms and foreign governments seeking to buy or represent U.S. products and services. U.S. Commercial Officers worldwide gather leads through local channels.

Lead details, such as specifications, quantities, end-use, delivery, and bid deadlines, are delivered daily to Washington, and then made available electronically within 24 hours directly to the U.S. business community in both printed and electronic form through private sector nationwide distributors. To contact the Economic Bulletin Board for electronic distribution call (202) 377-1986 or FAX (202) 377-2164. To try EBB as a guest user with your personal computer call (202) 377-3870 (8 bit words, no parity, 1 stop bit). Both new and established exporters can use TOP as a fundamental sales tool.

Contact: Trade Opportunities Program (TOP), International Trade Administration, United States and Foreign Commercial Service, Department of Commerce, 14th & Constitution Avenue NW, Washington, DC 20230. Phone (202) 377-2432, or 377-4767.

Credit and Other Info on Foreign Firms

Two sources of background information on foreign firms are the World Traders Data Reports and the Eximbank.

The World Traders Data Reports (WTDRs) are provided on individual foreign firms, containing information about each firm's business activities, its standing in the local business community, its credit-worthiness, and its overall reliability and suitability as a trade contract for U.S. exporters.

WTDRs are designed to help U.S. firms locate and evaluate potential foreign customers before making a business commitment.

A typical WTDR includes: name, address, and key contact, number of employees, type of business, general reputation in trade and financial circles, an assessment of the firm's suitability as a trade contact, year established, sales territory, and products handled.

Compiled by U.S. Commercial Officers abroad, WTDRs reflect their knowledge of local firms and business practices and include an evaluation of a company's suitability as a trade contract. In addition to normal checks with banks, trade and financial references, corporate and public records, local credit agencies and customers, the embassy uses its own files and contacts to compile each report.

In many less-developed countries, where even routine commercial information can be hard to get, WTDRs offer an excellent alternative to the difficult and painstaking task of acquiring information through individual contacts.

Contact: WTDRs, International Trade Administration, United States and Foreign Commercial Service, Department of Commerce, 14th & Constitution Avenue NW, Washington, DC 20230. Phone (202) 377-2432, or 377-4767.

Credit information of exceptional value is also available from the Eximbank to the commercial banking community and U.S. exporting firms in the financing of export sales to a specific country or individual company abroad.

To date, this has been one of the many resources of the Export-Import Bank that has not been utilized to full advantage. In keeping with traditional business practices, Eximbank will not divulge confidential financial data on foreign buyers to whom it has extended credit, nor will it disclose classified or confidential information regarding particular credits or conditions in foreign countries. However, the experience as related to repayment records of companies or countries with which Eximbank has done business can have a definite bearing on a decision to pursue certain export transactions overseas.

In addition, Eximbank is in a position to obtain additional information through its association with the banking and exporting community and other international agencies whose reviews might be helpful in determining if the export financing project should be undertaken.

The principal targets in Eximbank's campaign to furnish good credit data are the smaller exporters and commercial banks with limited international trade facilities.

Contact: Export-Import Bank of the United States, 811 Vermont Avenue NW, Washington, DC 20571. Phone (202) 566-4690.

Information on Fisheries in Foreign Countries

The **Foreign Fisheries Analysis Program** monitors marine fisheries around the world. It collects, evaluates, and distributes information on the latest political, economic, and scientific developments in world fisheries that affects the U.S. fishing industry or U.S. Government policies and programs.

The division also provides information concerning international shrimp and salmon aquaculture developments.

Contact: National Oceanic and Atmospheric Administration, National Marine Fisheries Service, Department of Commerce, 1335 East-West Highway, Silver Spring, MD 20910. Phone (301) 443-8910 or 427-2286.

Domestic and Foreign Fisheries Market News

The **Market News Program** offers current information on prices, market conditions, landings, imports, exports, cold-storage holdings, and market receipts of fishery products.

Information is collected by market reporters, and compiled and disseminated by Market News offices in Boston, New York, New Orleans, Terminal Island, and Seattle. The information aids U.S. buyers and sellers of fishery products in making intelligent marketing decisions.

Also reported is ancillary information such as innovations in harvesting, production, marketing, packaging and storage of fishery products, Federal fishery regulations and legislation, Regional Fishery Management Council meetings and activities, foreign fishing activities, foreign market information, and fishery meetings.

Contact: Market News Program, National Oceanic and Atmospheric Administration, National Marine Fisheries Service, Department of Commerce, 1335 East-West Highway, Silver Spring, MD 20910. Phone (301) 443-8910 or 427-2272.

Counseling on Bi-National Technological Joint Ventures

Information and counseling is available for those interested in establishing bi-national technology-oriented joint ventures. Experience with the successful U.S.-Israeli bi-national **Industrial Research and Development Program** is used as the basis.

The service focuses on higher technology and smaller businesses which have little knowledge of how to expand into operations abroad.

Contact: International Operations, Office of Technology Commercialization, Department of Commerce, 14th & Constitution Avenue NW, Room 4418, Washington, DC 20230. Phone Susan M. Lipsky at (202) 975-3690.

Legal Assistance on Duty Refunds

Refund assistance in the form of drawback is a provision of law by which a lawfully collected duty or tax is refunded or remitted, wholly or partially, because of a particular use made of the commodity on which the duty or tax was collected.

It encourages U.S. exporters by permitting them to compete in foreign markets without the handicap of including in the sales price the duty paid on the imported merchandise.

Since the exporter must know, before making contractual commitments, that he or she will be entitled to drawback on the exports, the drawback procedure is designed to give exporters this assurance and protection.

Drawback is payable to the exporter unless the manufacturer reserves the right to claim the refund. Several types of drawback are authorized under 19 U.S. C. 1313.

For more information, ask for the pamphlet *Drawback—A Duty Refund on Certain Exports* from any Government Printing Office bookstore or from the office below.

Contact: Entry Rulings Branch, U.S. Customs, Department of the Treasury, 1301 Constitution Avenue NW, Washington, DC 20229. Phone (202) 566-5856.

Free Legal Consultations for Exporters

Under an agreement with the Federal Bar Association, exporters with questions about international trade can receive free, initial legal consultation with an experienced trade attorney. Local, private attorneys around the country volunteer their time to assist small business exporters. Questions that can be addressed include:

- selling overseas

- getting paid

- licensing agreements

- joint ventures

- export regulations

- domestic and foreign taxation

- dispute resolution.

Contact: U.S. Small Business Administration, Office of International Trade, 409 Third Street, SW, 6th Floor, Washington, DC 20416.

If You've Been Hurt by Unfair Foreign Trade Practice

The **Trade Remedy Assistance Office** provides information on remedies and benefits available under trade laws and on the procedures necessary to obtain these benefits. For example, if you produce an item in competition with an item being imported and imports are increasing as to be a substantial cause of serious economic injury to the domestic market, a tariff adjustment or import quota may be imposed.

Affected firms and workers can also apply for financial assistance.

If a foreign government is subsidizing a product, you can petition for a countervailing duty to be imposed on the product.

If a foreign company is selling merchandise at less than fair value (dumping) in the U.S., anti-dumping duties may be imposed. Also technical assistance and informal legal advice is provided.

Contact: Trade Remedy Assistance Office, International Trade Commission, 500 E Street SW, Room 317, Washington, DC 20436. Phone (202) 205-2200 or (800) 343-7822.

Investment Opportunities Overseas

Two programs run by the Overseas Private Investment Corporation (a government agency) are the **Investor Information Service** and the **Opportunity Bank**.

For American businesses considering overseas ventures, obtaining basic information about foreign countries and their business environments is an important first step. Unfortunately, this is frequently a difficult and time-consuming process, given the variety of potential information sources and the resulting research required.

● **Investor Information Service**

> To assist U.S. firms in gathering such information, as well as facilitate the flow of information about developing countries to potential U.S. investors, OPIC has created the **Investor Information Service (IIS)**. IIS is a publications clearinghouse that provides interested companies and individuals with easy one-stop shopping for basic data and information commonly sought when considering investment overseas.

The materials, which are assembled into kit form, have been obtained from various U.S. Government agencies, foreign governments and international organizations. Together these source materials cover the economies, trade laws, business regulations and attitudes, political conditions, and investment incentives of specific developing countries and areas.

The information kits packaged by IIS are categorized by individual countries as well as major geographic regions and are sold for a nominal fee. At present, IIS kits are available for more than 110 developing countries and 16 regions.

● Opportunity Bank

A major stumbling block in the Third World's attempt to attract U.S. investment capital arises from the limited flow of information between potential U.S. equity investors and likely sponsors of investment projects in the developing countries. In its continuing effort to promote U.S. direct investment in the developing nations, OPIC has sought to establish channels of investment information by developing a computerized data system called the **Opportunity Bank**.

The primary purpose of this data bank is to enable U.S. firms and overseas project sponsors to register their respective investment interests and requirements, thus permitting rapid access to this information by interested potential joint-venture partners in the United States and abroad.

Currently, the Opportunity Bank contains more than 1,000 investment project profiles on a broad cross-section of potential joint-venture enterprises in more than 75 countries in the developing world. The company file contains more than 4,000 potential U.S. investors.

The OPIC Opportunity Bank is now available "on-line" through Mead Data Control's Lexis/Nexis services. Please call up "OPIC" when in the "WORLD" library of Nexis. Lexis/Nexis customer support can be reached at (800) 543-6862. For more information on these programs, contact: Overseas Private Investment Corporation, 1615 M Street NW, Washington, DC 20527. Phone (800) 424-6742. For businesses in Washington, DC call (202) 457-7010.

Foreign-trade Zones in the United States

Exporters should consider the use of **foreign trade zones** located in over 35 communities in the U.S. These zones are considered outside customs territory.

Activities such as storage, assembly, inspection, and repacking, which might otherwise be carried on overseas, are permitted.

For export operations the zones provide accelerated export status for excise tax rebates and customs drawbacks.

Contact: Office of Executive Secretary, Foreign Trade Zones Board, Room 3716, 14th & Pennsylvania Avenue NW, Washington, DC 20230. Phone John DaPonte at (202) 377-2862.

Matchmaker Trade Delegation Program

The matchmaker **Trade Delegation Program** is cosponsored by the Department of Commerce and the SBA. The missions are designed to introduce new-to-export or new-to-market businesses to prospective agents and distributors overseas. Commerce plans and organized about 10 missions a year. Each Matchmaker focuses on a specific industry or group of industries. SBA provides up to $750 of assistance to the first 10 qualified small businesses to sign up for each event. Specialists from the Department of Commerce evaluate the potential of a firm's product, find and screen potential business partners, and handle logistics. This is followed by an intensive trip filled with face-to-face meetings with prospective clients and in-depth briefings on the economic and business climate of the countries visited.

Contact: The SBA district office nearest you or; U.S. Office of International Trade, 409 Third Street, SW, 6th Floor, Washington, DC 20416

Advice for Exporters

If you are planning to add International Trade to your profit picture, be advised of two important items:

- the State Department, the Commerce Department, the U.S. Embassies abroad, and various specific-country trade missions have "country desks" and/or commercial attaches that are specialists in business conditions in the very country of your choice. A list of country desk officers is contained in Appendix 3

- each foreign country has different cultures, habits, customs and mores, and you better study up on them before you venture forth and make personal contact with their business or government representatives.

To learn more about foreign cultures, check out Roger E. Axtell's ***Do's and Taboos Around the World***, published by John Wiley & Sons for $10.95. You should know, too, that doing joint-venturing abroad will certainly expedite your contacts and improve relationships, rather than going the way of an American-owned subsidiary. Your own cultural biases, too, belong here, and should be exported abroad. Example: when you sign a business paper and pass it on to your Arabian counterpart, do so with your right hand, never with your left one. In the Middle East, Asia, and South America, it is considered uncouth to rush negotiations. Social amenities come first; business comes later.

Chapter 9

Women, Minorities, and Disadvantaged

Short-Term Lending and Bonding Assistance

The **Minority Business Resource Center** of the Department of Transportation operates two programs for minority, women-owned, and disadvantaged business enterprises:

- **The Short-Term Lending Program,** which provides short-term working capital at prime interest rates for transportation-related projects.

- **The Bonding Assistance Program,** which enables businesses to obtain bids, payment, and performance bonds for transportation-related projects.

For a minimal fee, these programs will also assist in the loan packaging.

Contact: Office of Small and Disadvantaged Business Utilization (OSDBU), Department of Transportation,

Minority Business Resource Center, 400 7th Street SW, Room 9414, Washington, DC 20590. Phone (202) 366-1930.

Information Networks

A nationwide **Business Information Network** has been established by the Minority Business Development Agency of the Department of Commerce. It collects and disseminates information that is of special importance to the successful establishment and operation of minority business.

The Network is comprised of 100 Minority Business Development Centers throughout the country, and the MBDA Information Clearinghouse Center.

The Centers are linked together through a telecommunications network and use remote terminals to access automated business information systems.

Information Clearinghouse

Services available from the clearinghouse are:

- Referral to sources of management and technical assistance for minority entrepreneurs.

- Identification of minority vendors for government agency procurement opportunities.

- Statistics and reports on Agency performance.

- Information about the Agency and other Federal support of minority assistance programs.

- Referral to and use of information resources at the Clearinghouse Reference Room.

Business Development Centers

Resources available through the Business Development Centers are:

- The Minority Vendor PROFILE System, which is a computerized inventory of non-retail minority firms used for matching companies with opportunities.

- The X/Market database containing information on approximately 500,000 U.S. establishments in more than 950 industries, used in making decisions concerning marketing, sales and research.

- Dun and Bradstreet Information Systems, which provides detailed financial profiles and computations useful in evaluating the performance of companies.

- DMS/ONLINE Information Systems which contains information on U.S. Government prime contract awards and plans for defense and aerospace programs and for identifying direct subcontracting opportunities for minority businesses.

- The TECTRA database that identifies new technologies being used in the public sector that are thus available for commercialization.

- The Donnelly X/Census Plus database that identifies desired characteristics of a given marketing location, and can also be searched to identify a location that meets these characteristics.

- The Federal Procurement Data System reports on various aspects of Federal procurement activities showing historical data on what the U.S. Government buys, used by many firms to develop marketing strategies.

- The F. W. Dodge Construction Information subscription service that provides information to minority business persons on both private and public sector construction opportunities, including post-construction services such as maintenance and landscaping.

More than 100 Minority Business Development Centers, located in areas across the country with the largest minority populations, are funded to provide management, marketing, and technical assistance to increase business opportunities for minority entrepreneurs in the United States and foreign markets.

Each center can assist existing firms as well as minority individuals interested in starting a business, and minimize their business failures.

The centers provide vital accounting, administration, business planning, construction, and marketing information. The sources of the information are major U.S. corporations, trade associations, export management companies, and Federal, state and local government agencies.

They also identify minority-owned firms for contract and sub-contract opportunities with Federal, state and local government agencies and the private sector. Some of the services include:

- financial statement compilation

- cost accounting

- budgeting; tax planning

- loan proposals

- cash forecasting

- office management

- form design

- management development

- job evaluation

- performance reviews

- feasibility studies

- long-range planning

- pre-merger analysis

- operation analysis

- construction bonding and estimating

- bid preparation

- pricing policies

- advertising

- promotion

- consumer surveys

- merchandising.

Businesses should contact their nearest MBDA regional office. To find it look in the telephone book or contact Minority Business Development Agency, Department of Commerce, 14th & Constitution Avenue NW, Washington, DC 20230. Phone (202) 377-1936.

Telecommunications Opportunities for Minorities

Engineering and management assistance is provided by the **Minority Telecommunications Development Program** to increase minority participation in all phases of telecommunications.

Through this program, minority business persons, educational institutions, and organizations are assisted in the creation and expansion of telecommunications businesses.

The MTDP helps minority entrepreneurs through a variety of initiatives:

- providing through its broadcast technical services project, initial engineering assistance in starting a broadcast facility

- analyzing and participating in industry developments, legislative and regulatory policymaking, and FCC proceedings to ensure that policies will adequately consider minority interests

- holding seminars and briefing for minority entrepreneurs and other organizations interested in business, manufacturing, and ownership opportunities available in telecommunications.

The MTDP has assembled three kits—commercial, noncommercial, and new technologies—to explain the services provided and also to inform minorities of the options and resources available in developing a telecommunications business. The kits provide:

- Information on the Technical Planning Services (TPS) component which assists minority entrepreneurs in the initial steps of developing commercial and noncommercial television and radio stations

- information handouts on starting commercial television and radio stations, cable systems, and a model financial proposal for the entrepreneur

- fact sheets on opportunities in the newer technologies

- sources for funding opportunities and technical assistance

- directories and general listings on assistance available.

Contact: Minority Telecommunications Development Program, National Telecommunications and Information

Administration, Department of Commerce, 14th & Constitution Avenue NW, Room 4725, Washington, DC 20230. Phone (202) 377-1880.

Energy-Related Opportunities for Minorities

The **Minority Energy Information Clearinghouse** is a centralized repository and dissemination point for energy-related research data and information about energy programs and the economic impact of those programs on minorities, minority businesses, and minority educational institutions. Information is provided about the Department of Energy (DOE) and the Office of Minority Economic Impact's (MI) Programs.

The clearinghouse maintains a database and provides searches and specialized information that is available through linkages with other databases of other Federal agencies.

Services available from the clearinghouse are:

- Referrals to sources of management and an array of technical assistance to minority business enterprises and minority educational institutions and to sources for procurement and research opportunities

- Identification of minority vendors for government procurement opportunities

- Statistics and performance reports on the Department's activities with minority educational institutions and minority business enterprises

- Information about DOE and other Federal agencies' support of minority assistance programs

- Identification of the research in progress in the Department

- Information on the impact of energy policies and programs on minorities

- Regional information on socioeconomic and demographic data on minorities and their energy use patterns, and

- Referrals to sources which assist in energy development programs for minority communities.

The clearinghouse has a bulletin board you can access from your personal computer via a modem. It contains numerous programs that impact minorities. The bulletin board is menu driven. It is available 24 hours a day. Call (800) 543-2325. The computer number is (202) 586-1561. For assistance call (202) 586-5876. The required modem setup is 1200 baud, 8 data bits, no parity, one stop bit, full duplex.

Contact: Minority Economic Impact Office, Department of Energy, 1000 Independence Avenue SW, Room 5B-110, Washington, DC 20585. Phone (202) 586-5876.

Business Loans and Grants for Indians and Alaska Natives

The **Bureau of Indian Affairs** will provide grants, direct loans and guaranteed loans for business, agriculture, industry and housing for Indians, Alaska natives, and Indian organizations.

Any purpose that will promote economic development on or near a Federal Indian Reservation will be considered. In 1992 approximately $45,000,000 is available for loan guarantees. Some recent projects were construction of a Dairy Queen, a cabinet factory, and a fish processing plant.

In addition, seed money in the form of grants up to $100,000 to individuals or $250,000 to tribes is available for profit-oriented business enterprises. One recent grant was for $40,000 to purchase a pizza parlor. The business is flourishing and they have expanded into a second restaurant without government assistance.

Contact: Trust and Economic Development, Bureau of Indian Affairs, 18th & C Streets NW, Room 4600, Washington, DC 20240. Phone Ray Quinn or Eugene Carneite at (202) 343-1400, 343-3657, or 382-1648.

Grants for Energy Usage Research

Money is available for research by minorities of energy usage such as: studies of the percentage of disposable income spent by minorities on energy compared to national averages, establishing consumption and usage patterns, and assessing potential policies and programs to be implemented by legislative and regulatory agencies.

Small and disadvantaged businesses in energy related fields are encouraged to apply.

Contact: Department of Energy, Forrestal Building Room 5B-110, Washington, DC 20585. Phone Georgia R. Johnson at (202) 586-1593 or 586-5876.

How to Contact Offices of Small and Disadvantaged Business Utilization (OSDBUs)

Department of Agriculture

The procurement procedures of the Department are explained by contacting the office. A special publication contains information on who does the buying, the types of items bought for the various programs, and where the buying is done. Included is a directory of purchasing offices and their locations.

Copies are available from this office. Information about contracting and subcontracting opportunities is also provided.

Contact: OSDBU, Department of Agriculture, 14th & Independence Avenue SW, Room 124-W, Washington, DC 20250. Phone (202) 447-7117.

Department of Commerce

The OSDBU provides individual and group marketing assistance for small businesses and publishes a forecast of Commerce contracting opportunities for the current year and a complete list of previous year contracts. Requisitions are screened for possible small business set-asides and the 8(a) program prior to publication in the Commerce Business Daily (CBD).

Each year the office sets goals for contracting and subcontracting awards to small, minority, 8(a) and women-owned businesses. They also review all prime contracts for subcontracting opportunities for these firms. For Commerce, the OSDBU administers *Small Business Innovation Research* and *R&D Goaling* programs and maintains a computer listing of small concerns wishing to do business with Commerce, the U.S. Government, and prime contractors.

Contact: OSDBU, Department of Commerce, Room H6411, 14th & Constitution Avenue NW, Washington, DC 20230. Phone Mr. James P. Maruca at (202) 377-3387.

Department of Defense

The OSDBU office is the starting point for small businesses, small disadvantaged businesses, labor surplus, and women-owned business firms desiring to do business with DOD.

A series of publications are available to lead a business to the right contacts with the large DOD procurement system. The key publications available include: *Selling to the Military, Department of Defense Small Business and Labor-Surplus Area Specialists,* and *Small Business Subcontracting Directory*.

Contact: OSDBU, Department of Defense, Room 2A340, The Pentagon, Washington, DC 20301-3061. Phone (202) 697-1481 or 614-1151.

Department of Education

The procurement procedures of the Department are explained by contacting the OSDBU office.

A special publication contains information on who does the buying, the types of items bought for the various programs, and where the buying is done. Included is a directory of purchasing offices and their locations. Copies are available from this office.

Contact: OSDBU, Department of Education, Room 6000, 555 New Jersey Avenue NW, Washington, DC 20202. Phone (202) 219-2050.

Department of Energy

The OSDBU office is the advocate and point of contact for small, disadvantaged (including 8a certified) firms, labor surplus areas and women-owned businesses.

The office counsels such firms on how to do business with the department. They also provide the names of small/disadvantaged business specialists located in the procurement offices throughout the country who can supply more specific requirement information. Preference programs are explained and potential vendors are referred to appropriate program offices.

Contact: OSDBU, Department of Energy, MA-41, 1000 Independence Avenue SW, Washington, DC 20585. Phone (202) 586-8201 or 254-5602.

Department of Health and Human Services

The OSDBU office develops and implements appropriate outreach programs aimed at heightening the awareness of the small business community to the contracting opportunities available within the Department.

Outreach efforts include activities such as sponsoring small business fairs and procurement conferences as well as participating in trade group seminars, conventions, and other forums which promote the utilization of small and disadvantaged businesses as contractors.

The OSDBU provides counseling and advice to inquiring small businesses regarding their possible eligibility for special consideration under preferential procurement programs for the Department employs.

Contact: OSDBU, Department of Health and Human Services, Room 513-D HHH, 200 Independence Avenue SW, Washington, DC 20201. Phone (202) 245-7300.

Department of Housing and Urban Development (HUD)

The OSDBU office helps small, minority, and women-owned businesses understand HUD's operations and directs offerers to appropriate sources of information. OSDBU works with program offices throughout the Department to develop goals for Procurement Opportunity Programs (POPs), Minority Business Enterprises (MBEs), and to encourage implementation of subcontracting plans for small and disadvantaged businesses.

It provides advice to contracting officers in complying with small and disadvantaged business utilization plans. The office participates in government/industry conferences to assist small and disadvantaged businesses and is available to give direct advice, as it is needed.

In addition, the office sponsors seminars and presentations at appropriate trade shows, conferences, and policy sessions.

OSDBU develops the Department's annual Minority Business Development Plan to encourage greater participation by minority business enterprises in all HUD programs.

Contact: OSDBU, Department of Housing and Urban Development, Room 10226, 451 Seventh Street SW, Washington, DC 20410. Phone (202) 708-3350.

Department of Justice

The OSDBU office develops and implements appropriate outreach programs aimed at heightening the awareness of the small business community to the contracting opportunities available within the Department.

Outreach efforts include activities such as sponsoring small business fairs and procurement conferences as well as participating in trade group seminars, conventions, and other forums which promote the utilization of small businesses as contractors.

The OSDBU also provides counseling and advice to inquiring small businesses regarding their possible eligibility for special consideration under preferential purchasing programs which the Department employs.

Contact: OSDBU, Department of Justice, 10th Street and Pennsylvania Avenue NW, Washington, DC 20530. Phone (202) 724-6271.

Department of Labor

The department places a fair proportion of its private sector purchases and contracts for supplies, research and development, and services (including contracts for maintenance, repairs, and construction) with small business and small disadvantaged business concerns.

The OSDBU office promotes opportunities for small business and disadvantaged business concerns in acquisition programs, disseminates information about those laws administered by the Department which affect contractor and subcontractor operations, and provides assistance to small and disadvantaged business concerns either directly or through coordinated interdepartmental activities.

The procurement procedures of the Department are explained in a publication titled *What the U.S. Department of Labor Buys*. This publication contains information on who does the buying, the types of items bought for the various programs, and where the buying is done. Included is a directory of purchasing offices and their locations. A copy is available from this office.

Contact: OSDBU, Department of Labor, Room N5402, 200 Constitution Avenue NW, Washington, DC 20210. Phone (202) 523-6481.

Department of the Interior

The OSDBU office is the central point of contact for small businesses, small disadvantaged businesses, labor surplus, and woman-owned business firms desiring to do business with the Department. The office is prepared to discuss the various preference programs and can assist firms in contacting appropriate Department offices.

Contact: OSDBU, Department of the Interior, 1849 C Street NW, Room 2727 Washington, DC 20240. Phone (202) 208-3493.

NASA

The OSDBU office (Code K) is responsible for the development and management of NASA programs to assist small businesses, as well as firms which are owned and controlled by socially and economically disadvantaged individuals.

The office functionally oversees and directs the activities of corresponding offices at each installation.

The primary objective of the program is to increase the participation of small and disadvantaged businesses in NASA procurement.

The office offers individual counseling sessions to business people seeking advice on how to best pursue contracting opportunities with NASA.

Specific guidance is provided regarding procedures for getting on the bidders' mailing lists, current and planned procurement opportunities, arrangements for meetings with technical requirements personnel, and various assistance or preference programs which might be available.

Contact: OSDBU, National Aeronautics and Space Administration, Code K, Washington, DC 20546. Phone Mr. Eugene D. Rosen at (202) 453-2088.

Department of Transportation

The OSDBU office provides assistance, referrals, and business opportunity information resulting from the Department's Federally assisted projects to minority and women business enterprises through its nationwide Program Management Center Project, Hispanic Business Enterprise Project, and National Information Clearinghouse.

It provides assistance in obtaining short-term capital and bonding for minority and women business enterprises.

The MBRC contracts annually with a number of organizations to assist minority and women business enterprises in obtaining contracts from Federally assisted projects.

Contact: OSDBU, Department of Transportation, Room 9414, 400 7th Street SW, Washington, DC 20590. Phone (202) 366-1930.

Department of the Treasury

The OSDBU office is a central point of contact for small business, small disadvantaged business, labor surplus and women-owned business firms desiring to do business with the Treasury.

OSDBU is prepared to discuss the various procurement programs and can assist firms in contacting appropriate Treasury procurement personnel.

Contact: OSDBU, Department of the Treasury, Main Treasury Building, 15th and Pennsylvania Avenue NW,

Room 6100 Annex, Washington, DC 20220. Phone Ms.
Debra E. Sonderman at (202) 566-9616.

General Services Administration

Assistance: Information/Marketing/Networking

The eleven GSA Business Service Centers provide small and
disadvantaged businesses with detailed information about
Government contracting opportunities. They issue bidders'
mailing list applications, furnish specifications and
invitations for bids, maintain current displays of bidding
opportunities, receive and safeguard bids and provide
facilities for opening them, and furnish copies of publications
designed to assist business representatives in doing business
with the Government. Copies of bid abstracts—which
indicate successful bidders, other bidders, and prices
bid—are also available.

The GSA publication, Doing Business *With the Federal
Government*, explains basic procurement policies and
procedures of GSA, the Department of Defense, and 16 other
agencies and contains the locations and telephone numbers of
GSA Business Service Centers and 100 GSA Small Business
Information Offices across the country. It is available free
from a Business Service Center. Each regional center
publishes a procurement directory for the area it serves.

Contact: General Services Administration, Room 6017, 18th
& F Street, NW, Washington, DC 20405. Telephone: (202)
566-1021.

Programs for Women

A women-owned business is defined as a "business that is at
least 51%-owned by a woman or women, who also controls
and operates it." Women are not classified as minorities for
Federal SBA programs; however, some states do classify
women as minorities and they are therefore eligible for state
programs.

Since 1977, SBA has had an ongoing nationwide women's business ownership program. A Women in Business Representative, represents the **Women's Business Ownership Program**, that sponsors special programs for women business owners and those interested in starting their own businesses.

In 1983, SBA began organizing a series of Regional conferences that focus on such topics as business expansion, while local training programs cover general business topics of specialized areas such as home-based businesses, franchising or selling to the Federal government.

SBA announced in March 1990, nine new initiatives to help increase business ownership opportunities for women:

- Improve access to credit for women-owned businesses

- Fully implement the "$50,000 or less" Small Loan Program

- Increase prime and subcontract awards to women-owned small businesses

- Establish the Women's Network for Entrepreneurial Training (WNET) Program in 50 States

- Increase representation of women on SBA's National and Regional Advisory Councils

- Increase recruitment and representation of women in key management and administrative positions at SBA

- Increase information about demographics, and

- Support the work of the National Women's Business Council.

Publication:

A *Women's Business Ownership Kit* is available from SBA, free. Fact Sheet #45, Women-Owned Businesses.

The **National Women's Business Council**, was established
by the Women's Business ownership Act of 1988, consists of
nine members, three of which are mandated by legislation
and six appointed by congressional leadership. According to
the Act, the Council reviews, reports, and recommends
actions in four specific areas:

● The status of women-owned businesses nationwide,
  including progress made and remaining barriers for
  assisting businesses in entering the mainstream of
  American economy.

● The roles of Federal, state and local governments in
  assisting and promoting women-owned businesses.

● Data collection procedures and the availability of data
  relating to women-owned businesses.

● Other government initiatives which may exist relating
  to women-owned businesses including Federal
  procurement.

Women's Business Ownership—Procurement Representatives (WOBREP)

● The following Federal agencies have Women-Owned
  Business Representatives: ask SBA for a local list.

Department of:

Agriculture	(202) 447-7117
Commerce	(202) 377-1472
Defense	(703) 697-1481
Army	(703) 697-2868
Air Force	(703) 697-5373

Navy	(703) 602-2695
Defense Logistics	(703) 274-6977
Education	(202) 708-9822
Energy	(202) 254-5602
Health & Human Services	(202) 245-2670
Housing & Urban Development	(202) 708-3350
Interior	(202) 208-7437
Justice	(202) 501-6271
Labor	(202) 523-9151
State	(703) 875-6824
Transportation	(202) 366-1902
Treasury	(202) 566-5704
Department of Veterans Affairs	(202) 376-6996

Independent Agencies

Action	(202) 634-9321
Agency for International Development	(703) 875-1551
Consumer Product Safety Commission	(301) 492-6570
Federal Maritime Commission	(202) 523-5900
Federal Trade Commission	(202) 326-2260
Interstate Commerce Commission	(202) 275-7597
National Endowment for Humanities	(202) 786-0233
National Science Foundation	(202) 357-7464
Office of Personnel Management	(202) 606-2240
Small Business Administration	(202) 205-6673
Smithsonian Institution	(202) 287-3343
Commodity Futures Trading Commission	(202) 254-9735
Environmental Protection Agency	(703) 557-7305
Federal Emergency Management Agency	(202) 646-3743

General Services Administration	(202) 501-1012
NASA	(202) 453-2088
National Labor Relations Board	(202) 634-4019
Nuclear Regulatory Commission	(301) 492-4667
Resolution Trust Corporation	(202) 416-7467
SBA Liaison Pentagon	(202) 695-2435
U.S. Postal Service	(202) 268-4633

Chapter 10

Odds and Ends

Answers to Questions on Truth in Advertising, Mail Order, Buying by Phone

The **Public Reference Branch** of the Federal Trade Commission answers questions concerning truthful advertising, price fixing, product warranties, truth in lending, and unfair and deceptive business acts. It offers business assistance in learning about current regulations and enforcement procedures.

Examples of common questions answered include: mail orders rules, buying by phone, FTC used car rules, getting business credit, handling customer complaints, how to advertise consumer credit, making business sense out of warranty law, and writing a care label.

Although major emphasis is placed on correcting unfair or deceptive business practices that hurt competition, businesses can also inform the Commission of unfair competition from monopolistic practices including price fixing, boycotts, price discrimination, and illegal mergers and acquisitions.

Ten regional FTC offices also have been established to assist businesses and consumers.

Contact: Public Reference Branch, Federal Trade Commission, Room 130, 6th & Pennsylvania Avenue NW, Washington, DC 20580. Phone (202) 326-2222.

Buying Surplus Goods

The Defense National Stockpile Center acquires and retains certain materials in order to prevent a dependence upon foreign nations in times of national emergency. Disposals are made when materials in inventory are found to be in excess of national security needs and, usually, are approved by Congress.

Disposals are conducted on a nonexclusive, nondiscriminatory basis by means of sealed bids, auctions, negotiations, or other sales methods.

Every reasonable effort is made to carry out a long-term acquisition and disposal plan as formally announced. This allows industry to make developmental, research, and investment plans in anticipation of these disposals.

Contact: Defense Logistics Agency, Defense National Stockpile Center (DNSC), 1745 Jefferson Davis Highway, Arlington, VA 22202-3402. Phone (703) 607-3218.

Buying Surplus Real Estate

The Federal Property Resource Service of the General Services Administration has the principal responsibility for surplus real property sales. It sells nearly every type of real estate found on the commercial market.

In many cases, buyers may use the properties immediately after they have been awarded the contract for purchase.

When Government real property is for sale, the GSA regional office prepares a notice describing the property and how it will be sold. The notice is mailed to those who have shown an interest in buying similar property.

A computerized mailing list is maintained, and bidders' applications are available at each of GSA's Business Service Centers.

Contact: Federal Property Resources Service, General Services Administration, Office of Real Property, 7th & D Streets SW, Room 5466, Washington, DC 20407. Phone toll-free 1-800-472-1313 or local (202) 501-0067.

Commodity Futures and How They Can Be Used to Control Costs

The Communications and Education Services Office of the Commodity Futures Trading Commission offers information about commodity futures and options to assist businesses in determining their value in company purchasing and marketing strategies.

Although only a small percentage of futures trading actually leads to delivery of a commodity, futures trading can be a valuable cost control method for companies.

The Commission regulates trading, offers information about futures, and works with business groups on new contracts or rule changes and to help educate them about these changes.

Contact: The Communication and Education Service Office, Commodity Futures Trading Commission, 2033 K Street NW, Washington, DC 20581. Phone (202) 254-8630.

Management Assistance for Rural Co-Ops

The Agricultural Cooperative Service provides research, management, and educational assistance to cooperatives to strengthen the economic position of farmers and other rural residents.

It works directly with cooperative leaders and Federal and state agencies to improve organization, leadership, and operation of cooperatives and to give guidance to further development.

It helps;

- farmers and other rural residents develop cooperatives to obtain supplies and services at lower costs and to get better prices for products they sell

- advises rural residents on developing existing resources through cooperative action to enhance rural living

- helps cooperatives improve services and operating efficiency

- informs members, directors, employers, and the public on how co-operatives work and benefit their members and their communities

- encourages international cooperative programs.

The agency publishes research and educational materials, and issues *Farmer Cooperatives*, a monthly periodical.

Contact: Agricultural Cooperative Service, Department of Agriculture, Washington, DC 20250. Phone Dr. Randall E. Torgerson at (202) 245-5358.

Where to Get Answers on Energy Conservation and Creating Renewable Energy from Wind, Sun, Crops and Waste

The Conservation and Renewable Energy Inquiry and Referral Service (CAREIRS) provides basic information on the full spectrum of renewable energy technologies—solar, wind, hydroelectric, photovoltaics, geothermal and bioconversion—and on energy conservation.

For requesters who need detailed assistance on technical problems, CAREIRS provides referrals to other organizations or publications. Its purpose is to aid technology transfer by responding to public inquiries on the use of renewable energy technologies and conservation techniques for residential and commercial needs.

Once an inquiry has been initiated, the response process is basically computerized. Responses consist of a form letter with applicable publications; an immediate telephone response; an occasional original draft response; or referral to other organizations.

Contact: CAREIRS, Department of Energy, P.O. Box 8900, Silver Spring, MD 20907. Call toll-free (800) 523-2929; in Alaska and Hawaii call (800) 233-3071.

Help with Labor Management Relations

Two programs can provide timely information and help.

● The **Cooperative Labor Management Program**, often identified as the Quality of Work Life program. It is a joint effort by labor and management to work together to further their mutual interests. The aim is more satisfied and involved employees and more efficient, adaptive, and productive organizations.

The program offers a wide range of information and technical assistance services including the sponsorship of conferences and symposia, the publication of reports on organizational experiences, the preparation of educational and training materials, and the conduct of research and evaluation studies.

There is particular interest in gathering and disseminating information about innovative policies and programs developed to enhance employee participation in decision-making with regard to such issues as work organization, the work environment, technological change, and plant closures.

The division works primarily with national unions, trade associations, productivity and quality of work life centers, colleges and universities, and other organizations interested in cooperative labor relations and quality of work life programs.

For more information on this, contact: Cooperative
Labor-Management Program, Department of Labor,
200 Constitution Avenue NW, Room N-5416,
Washington, DC 20210. Phone (202) 523-6098.

- The **Mediation and Conciliation Service**, which
  promotes labor-management peace and better
  labor-management relations by providing mediation
  assistance in disputes arising between organized
  employees and their employers. The service has 80
  field offices in cities across the United States.

  Businesses will find its services helpful in preventing or
  minimizing work stoppages; in helping to resolve
  collective bargaining disputes, by creating a better
  degree of understanding and cooperation between
  management and labor, and in assisting labor and
  management to select impartial arbitrators to hear and
  decide disputes over collective bargaining agreements.

  In general, assistance from the service is limited to
  domestic employers involved in interstate commerce
  and to related labor organizations. Except as a last
  resort, it refrains from participation in intrastate matters
  or in controversies pertaining to the interpretation or
  application of existing contracts. Services may be
  provided either upon notice required by law or at the
  request of the involved parties.

  The labor organizations involved must be recognized by
  the National Labor Relations Board as legitimate
  representatives of employee groups.

A series of films is also available. They illustrate many of
today's labor relations problems.

Contact: Federal Mediation and Conciliation Services, 2100
K Street NW, 9th Floor, Washington, DC 20427. Phone Mr.
James Power at (202) 653-5300.

Your Friend in
The Environmental Protection Agency

The EPA Small Business Ombudsman has the mission of;

● providing small businesses with easier access to the Agency

● helping them comply with environmental regulations; investigating and resolving small business disputes with the Agency

● increasing EPA's sensitivity to small business in developing regulations

● dealing with EPA enforcement policies, inspection procedures, and fines

● understanding water-permitting regulations and requirements for handling and treating hazardous wastes

● complying with registration procedures for pesticides

● information on financing for pollution control equipment.

They answer all kinds of questions, too. For instance, do you want to import an automobile? Ask them about emissions requirements. Need some bacterial cultures for lab research? They'll send some from their lab. Can't understand the government's EPA rules? They'll have one of their people walk you through it.

A major responsibility of the Ombudsman is to follow closely the status and development of EPA policies affecting small businesses. The Ombudsman's office can help provide the latest information on new regulations. Several EPA brochures and reports on various small business activities and environmental issues also are available.

Contact: EPA Small Business Ombudsman, Environmental Protection Agency, 401 M Street SW (A-149C), Washington, DC 20460. Call Karen V. Brown toll-free at (800) 368-5888, or from within the Washington DC area at (202) 557-1938.

Impartial Information on Pesticides

The National Pesticide Telecommunications Network provides a variety of impartial information about pesticides to anyone in the contiguous United States, Puerto Rico, and the Virgin Islands. It provides the medical community health professional with:

- pesticide product information

- information on recognition and management of poisonings

- toxicology and symptomatic reviews

- It gives referrals for laboratory analyses, investigations of pesticide incidents, and emergency treatment information.

The general public is also provided pesticide information ranging from:

- product information

- protective equipment

- safety, health and environmental effects

- clean-up procedures, disposal, and regulatory laws.

Contact: National Pesticides Telecommunications Network, Environmental Protection Agency, Texas Tech University, Health Sciences Center, Department of Preventive Medicine, Lubbock, TX 79430. Call toll-free (800) 858-7378.

Assistance Concerning Hazardous Wastes

The Hazardous Waste/Superfund Hotline was created because the Environmental Protection Agency recognized:

- that many of the firms which must comply with regulations would have difficulty understanding the regulations and the statutory requirements

- that many of these firms, particularly the smaller ones, were not in a financial position to hire consultants to answer their compliance questions

- that interested communities, including private citizens, may have questions.

The Hotline serves as a central source of technical information on the Superfund Program and the Hazardous Waste Management Program.

The Hotline responds to approximately 20,000 calls per month on regulations and program activities. In addition, the Hotline telephone service accepts requests for related publications. When additional information is required, the Hotline refers callers to appropriate contacts at EPA Headquarters, EPA Regional offices, and other Federal and state agencies. The Hotline telephone staff has ten information specialists with background in geology, chemistry, chemical and environmental engineering, hydrogeology, biology, and environmental science.

Contact: Hazardous Wastes/Superfund Hotline, Environmental Protection Agency, 401 M Street SW, Mail Code 05-305, Washington, DC 20460. Call toll-free (800) 424-9346 or in Washington, DC (202) 382-3000.

Crime Insurance for Small Businesses

The Federal Crime Insurance Program makes crime insurance available in states where it has been determined that this insurance is not fully available at affordable rates.

This Federally subsidized program was created to make crime insurance more readily available in areas where people have been unable to buy or renew crime insurance protection from the private insurance market. Policies normally will not be cancelled or non-renewed because the policyholder has reported losses.

Coverage for business is available in increments of $1,000 up to a maximum of $15,000 with a choice of the following policy coverage:

Option 1: Burglary only, including safe burglary, and resulting damage.

Option 2: Robbery only, inside and away from the premises, and resulting damage.

Option 3: A combination of burglary and robbery in uniform and varying amounts.

Contact: Federal Crime Insurance Program, Federal Insurance Administration, Federal Emergency Management Agency, P.O. Box 6301, Rockville, MD 20850. Call toll-free (800) 638-8780; businesses in Washington, DC or Maryland should call (301) 251-1660.

Computer Software You Can Have

The Computer Software and Management Information Center (COSMIC) makes available to business and industry over 1,200 computer programs covering all areas of NASA project involvement, including structural analysis, thermal engineering, computer graphics, image processing, controls and robotics, artificial intelligence and expert systems. Source code is supplied for each program along with detailed user documentation.

Contact: Pat Mortenson, Marketing Coordinator, COSMIC, National Aeronautics and Space Administration, University of Georgia, 382 E. Broad Street, Athens, GA 30602. Phone (404) 542-3265.

The Internet address is: service @ cossack.cosmic.uga.edu
(No, that's not a typographical error).

Audio Visual Programs Available for You

The National Audiovisual Center is the central distribution
source of audiovisual programs produced by the U.S.
Government. Companies interested in using video material
for training will find it useful to obtain copies of the center's
descriptive catalogs and brochures.

Some of the audiovisuals available cover: alcohol and drug
abuse, business/government management, consumer
education, dentistry, environment/energy conservation,
flight/meteorology, foreign language instruction, history,
industrial safety, library/information science, medicine,
nursing, science, social issues, special education, and
vocational education.

Contact: National Audiovisual Center, National Archives and
Records Administration, 8700 Edgeworth Drive, Capitol
Heights, MD 20743. Phone (301) 763-1896.

Help for Businesses in Protecting Pension Plans

The Communications and Public Affairs Department of
the Pension Benefit Guaranty Corporation (PBGC) will
explain how the PBGC protects the retirement incomes of
more than 38,000,000 American workers participating in
more than 112,000 covered private-sector benefit pension
plans.

The Corporation has assumed liability for payment of
guaranteed vested pension benefits to more than 193,000
participants in approximately 1,400 plans that have
terminated and are or will be trusteed by the PBGC, and is
currently paying monthly retirement benefits to more than
184,000 retirees. The amount of the monthly benefit that the
PBGC guarantees is set by law.

The PBGC administers two pension programs: the
single-employer program and the multi-employer program.

The single-employer program covers approximately 30,000,000 participants in about 110,000 single-employer pension plans.

When a single-employer plan insured by the PBGC terminates without sufficient funds to pay PBGC-guaranteed benefits, the PBGC makes up the difference, thus ensuring that all qualified participants and beneficiaries receive their guaranteed pensions.

The PBGC also assumes trusteeship of the plan and manages its assets, maintains the plan's records, and administers guaranteed benefits. The multi-employer program protects about 8,000,000 participants in more than 2,000 plans. Multi-employer pension plans are maintained under collective bargaining agreements and cover employees of two or more unrelated employers.

If PBGC-covered multi-employer plans become insolvent, they receive financial assistance from the PBGC to enable them to pay guaranteed benefits.

Contact: Communications and Public Affairs Department, Pension Benefit Guaranty Corporation, 2020 K Street NW, Washington, DC 20006-1806. Phone Mr. E. William FitzGerald at (202) 778-8839.

How to Request Securities and Exchange Commission Information

The Reference Assistance Program makes available Securities and Exchange Commission information collected when exercising its mandate concerning the protection of investors and the maintenance of fair and orderly securities markets. The Commission carries out its mandate under five principal laws. Under these Acts and the rules under them, publicly held corporations, broker-dealers in securities, investment companies and investment advisors must file information with the Commission. Filings are designed to ensure that all material information is available to the investing public in a timely fashion.

To ensure easy public access, the Commission maintains public reference rooms in New York, Chicago and in the headquarters office in Washington. During normal business hours, individuals may review and photocopy all public filings.

In addition, copies may be ordered by writing to the Commission or telephoning the Commission's contract copying service. The Commission will, upon written request, have copies of any public documents or information sent by mail. Companies or individuals must submit a written request stating the documents or information needed.

Further information should be obtained before writing and stating your willingness to pay the photocopying and shipping charges. Each request will take approximately two to three weeks for delivery.

For quicker service or in-depth research, it is suggested to employ one of the private firms which provide SEC research services. A list of these firms and additional information is available.

Contact: Reference Assistance Program, Securities and Exchange Commission, Public Reference Branch, Stop 1-2, 450 5th Street NW, Washington, DC 20549. Phone (202) 272-7450.

When Someone Complains about Your Business

The Office of Consumer Affairs provides assistance to businesses to help them improve customer relations. They have five consumer affairs guides for business:

Advertising, Packaging, and Labeling

Managing Consumer Complaints

Product Warranties and Services

Credit and Financial Issues

Consumer Product Safety.

They also present workshops based on these guides and have prepared manuals for use by the workshop coordinators and consumer protection agencies. Other publications useful to businesses are *Consumer Services Directory* and *Guide to Complaint Handling*.

To get more information, write or call: Office of Consumer Affairs, Patricia Faoro, Director, Department of Commerce, Room 5718, Office of the Secretary, Washington, DC 20230. Phone (202) 377-5001.

How to Get Help on Safety Without Getting into Trouble

Employers can receive a free confidential consultation to help recognize and correct safety and health hazards in their workplaces.

The service is delivered by a well-trained professional staff. Most consultations take place on-site, though limited services away from the worksite are available. Primarily targeted for smaller businesses, this confidential safety and health consultation program is completely separate from the OSHA inspection effort. In addition, no citations are issued or penalties imposed.

A consultant will study an entire plant or specific designated operations and discuss the applicable OSHA standards. Consultants also will point out other safety or health risks which might not be cited under OSHA standards, but which nevertheless may pose safety or health risks. They may suggest other measures such as self-inspection and safety and health training to prevent future hazardous situations.

A comprehensive consultation also includes:

- Appraisal of all mechanical and environmental hazards and physical work practices

- Appraisal of the present job safety and health program or establishment of one

- A conference with management on findings

- A written report of recommendations and agreements

- Training and assistance with implementing recommendations.

Contact: OSHA Consultation Program, Occupational Safety and Health Administration, Department of Labor, Room N-3700, 200 Constitution Avenue NW, Washington, DC 20210. Phone (202) 523-7266.

Appendix 1

Federal Information Centers

The Federal Information Center Program (FIC) is a one-stop source of assistance when you have a question of problem related to the Federal Government. The FIC will answer your question or assist you in finding the right office for the answer. For a more complete description of the service see Chapter 3.

Please call the number listed below for your metropolitan area or State. If your area is not listed, call (301) 722-9098 or write to Federal Information Center, P.O. Box 600, Cumberland, MD 21501-0600. Users of Telecommunications Devices for the Deaf (TDD/TTY) may call toll-free from any point in the United States by dialing (800) 326-2996.

Alabama:
Birmingham, Mobile   (800) 366-2998
Alaska:
Anchorage   (800) 729-8003
Arizona:
Phoenix   (800) 359-3997
Arkansas:
Little Rock   (800) 366-2998

California:
    Los Angeles, San Diego
    San Francisco, Santa Ana   (800) 726-4995
    Sacramento   (916) 973-1695
Colorado:
    Colorado Springs,
    Denver, Pueblo   (800) 359-3997
Connecticut:
    Hartford, New Haven   (800) 347-1997
Florida:
    Fort Lauderdale,
    Jacksonville, Miami,
    Orlando, St. Petersburg,
    Tampa, West Palm Beach   (800) 347-1997
Georgia:
    Atlanta   (800) 347-1997
Hawaii:
    Honolulu   (800) 733-5996
Illinois:
    Chicago   (800) 366-2998
Indiana:
    Gary   (800) 366-2998
    Indianapolis   (800) 347-1997
Iowa:
    All locations   (800) 735-8004
Kansas:
    All locations   (800) 735-8004
Kentucky:
    Louisville   (800) 347-1997
Louisiana:
    New Orleans   (800) 366-2998
Maryland:
    Baltimore   (800) 347-1997
Massachusetts:
    Boston   (800) 347-1997
Michigan:
    Detroit, Grand Rapids   (800) 347-1997
Minnesota:
    Minneapolis   (800) 366-2998
Missouri:
    St. Louis   (800) 366-2998
    All other locations   (800) 735-8004

Nebraska:
    Omaha   (800) 366-2998
    All other locations   (800) 735-8004
New Jersey:
    Newark, Trenton   (800) 735-8004
New Mexico:
    Albuquerque   (800) 359-1997
New York:
    Albany, Buffalo,
    New York, Rochester,
    Syracuse   (800) 347-1997
North Carolina:
    Charlotte   (800) 347-1997
Oklahoma:
    Oklahoma City, Tulsa   (800) 366-2998
Oregon:
    Portland   (800) 726-4995
Pennsylvania:
    Philadelphia, Pittsburgh   (800) 347-1997
Rhode Island:
    Providence   (800) 347-1997
Tennessee:
    Chattanooga   (800) 347-1997
    Memphis, Nashville   (800) 366-2998
Texas:
    Austin, Dallas, Fort Worth,
    Houston, San Antonio   (800) 366-2998
Utah:
    Salt Lake City   (800) 359-3997
Virginia:
    Norfolk, Richmond,
    Roanoke   (800) 347-1997
Washington:
    Seattle, Tacoma   (800) 726-4995
Wisconsin:
    Milwaukee   (800) 366-2998

Appendix 2

SBA FIELD OFFICES

Alabama
Suite 200
2121 8th Avenue N
Birmingham, AL 35203-2398
(205) 731-1344

Alaska
222 West 8th Avenue
Anchorage, AK 99513-7559
(907) 271-4005

Arizona
Suite 800
2828 N. Central Avenue
Phoenix, AZ 85004-1025
(602) 640-2316

300 W. Congress Street
Tucson, AZ 85701
(602) 670-4759

Arkansas
2120 Riverfront Drive
Little Rock, AR 72202
(501) 324-5278

California
660 J Street
Sacramento, CA 95814
(916) 551-1426

880 Front Street
San Diego, CA 92188-270
(619) 557-7252

4th Floor
211 Main Street
San Francisco, CA 94105
(415) 744-6820

20th Floor
71 Stevenson Street
San Francisco, CA 94105
(415) 774-6402

Suite 160
901 W. Civic Center Drive
Santa Ana, CA 92703
(714) 836-2200

Suite 10
6477 Telephone Road
Ventura, CA 93003
(805) 642-1866

Colorado
Suite 426
721 19th Street
Denver, CO 80202
(303) 844-3984

Connecticut
2nd Floor
330 Main Street
Hartford, CT 06106
(203) 240-4700

District Of Columbia
6th Floor
1111 18th Street, NW
Washington, DC 20036
(202) 634-1500

Delaware
Suite 412
920 N. King Street
Wilmington, DE 19801
(302) 573-6644

Florida
1320 S. Dixie Highway
Suite 501
Coral Gables, FL 33146
(305) 536-5521

Suite 100-B
7825 Baymeadows Way
Jacksonville, FL 32256-7504
(904) 443-1900

Suite 104
501 East Polk Street
Tampa, FL 33602-3945
(813) 228-2594

Suite 402
5601 Corporate Way
W. Palm Bch., FL 33407-2044
(407) 689-3922

Georgia
5th Floor
1375 Peachtree Street, NE
Atlanta, GA 30367-8102
(404) 347-2797

6th Floor
1720 Peachtree Rd., NW
Atlanta, GA 30309
(404) 347-4749

Room 225
52 N. Main Street
Statesboro, GA 30458
(912) 489-8719

Hawaii
300 Ala Moana Boulevard
Honolulu, HI 96850
(808) 541-3650

Idaho
1020 Main Street
Boise, ID 83702
(208) 334-1696

Illinois
Suite 1975
300 S. Riverside Plaza
Chicago, IL 60606-6617
(312) 353-0359

Room 1250
500 W. Madison Street
Chicago, IL 60661-2511
(312) 353-4528

Suite 302
511 W. Capitol Street
Springfield, IL 62704
(217) 492-4416

Indiana
Suite 100
429 N. Pennsylvania
Indianapolis, IN 46204-1873
(317) 226-7272

Iowa
Room 749
New Federal Building
210 Walnut Street
Des Moines, IA 50309
(515) 284-4422

Kansas
Suite 510
100 East English Street
Wichita, KS 67202
(316) 269-6273

Kentucky
Room 188
600 Dr. M.L.K. Jr. Pl
Louisville, KY 40202
(502) 582-5971

Louisiana
Suite 2000
1661 Canal Street
New Orleans, LA 70112
(504) 589-6685

Massachusetts
9th Floor
155 Federal Street
Boston, MA 02110
(617)451-2023

Room 265
10 Causeway Street
Boston, MA 02222-1093
(617) 565-5590

Room 212
1550 Main Street
Springfield, MA 01103
(413) 785-0268

Maryland
3rd Floor
10 N. Calvert Street
Baltimore, MD 21202
(410) 962-4392

Maine
Room 512
40 Western Avenue
Augusta, ME 04330
(207 622-8378

Michigan
Room 515
477 Michigan Avenue
Detroit, MI 48226
(313) 226-6075

228 West Washington St.
Marquette, MI 49885
(906) 225-1108

Minnesota
Suite 610
100 N. 6th Street
Minneapolis, MN
55403-1563
(612) 370-2324

Mississippi
Suite 1001
One Hancock Plaza
Gulfport, MS 39501-7758
(601) 863-4449

Suite 400
101 W. Capitol Street
Jackson, MS 39201
(601) 965-4378

Missouri
Suite 501
323 W. Eighth St.
Kansas City, MO 64105
(816) 374-6764

Room 242
815 Olive Street
St. Louis, MO 63101
(314) 539-6600

Montana
Room 528
301 S. Park
Helena, MT 59626
(406) 449-5381

Nebraska
11145 Mill Valley Road
Omaha, NE 68154
(402) 221-4691

Nevada
Room 301
301 E. Stewart Street
Las Vegas, NV 89125-2527
(702) 388-6611

North Carolina
200 N. College Street
Charlotte, NC 28202
(704) 344-6563

North Dakota
Room 218
Federal Building
657 2nd Avenue, North
Fargo, ND 58108-3086
(701) 239-5131

New Hampshire
Suite 202
143 N. Main Street
Concord, NH O3302-1257
(603) 225-1400

New Jersey
2600 Mt. Ephrain Ave
Camden, NJ 08104
(609) 757-5183

4th Floor
60 Park Place
Newark, NJ 07102
(201) 645-2434

New Mexico
625 Silver SW
Albuquerque, NM 87102
(505) 766-1870

New York
Room 815
Leo O'Brian Bldg.
Albany, NY 12207
(518) 472-6300

Room 1311
111 W. Huron Street
Buffalo, NY 14202
(716) 846-4301

4th Floor
333 E. Water Street
Elmira, NY 14901
(607) 734-8130

Room 102E
35 Pinelawn Road
Melville, NY 11747
(516) 454-0750

Room 3100
26 Federal Plaza
New York, NY 10278
(212) 264-1450

Room 3100
26 Federal Plaza
New York, NY 10278
(212) 264-1450

Room 410
100 State Street
Rochester, NY 14614
(716) 263-6700

Room 1071
100 S. Clinton Street
Syracuse, NY 13260
(315) 423-5383

Ohio
Suite 870
525 Vine Street
Cincinnati, OH 45202
(513) 684-2814

Room 317
1240 E. 9th Street
Cleveland, OH 44199
(216) 522-4180

Suite 1400
2 Nationwide Plaza
Columbus, OH 43215
(614) 469-6860

Oklahoma
Suite 670
200 N.W. 5th Street
Oklahoma City, OK 73102
(405) 231-4301

Oregon
Suite 500
222 S.W. Columbia
Portland, OR 97201
(503) 326-2682

Pacific Islands
20th Floor
71 Stevenson Street
San Francisco, CA 94105
(415) 774-6402

Pennsylvania
Room 309
100 Chestnut Street
Harrisburg, PA 17101
(717) 782-3840

Suite 201
475 Allendale Road
King Prussia, PA 19406
(215) 962-3804

5th Floor
960 Penn Avenue
Pittsburgh, PA 15222
(412) 644-2780

Room 2327
20 N. Pennsylvania Avenue
Wilkes-Barre, PA 18702
(717) 826-6497

Puerto Rico
Room 691
Carlos Chardon Avenue
Hato Rey, PR 00918
(809) 766-5572

Rhode Island
5th Floor
380 Westminster Mall
Providence, RI 02903
(401) 528-4561

South Carolina
Room 358
1835 Assembly Street
Columbia, SC 29201
(803) 765-5376

South Dakota
Suite 101
101 South Main Avenue
Sioux Falls, SD 57102-0527
(605) 330-4231

Tennessee
Suite 201
50 Vantage Way
Nashville, TN 37228-1500
(615) 736-5881

Texas
Suite 1200
606 N. Carancahua
Corpus Christi, TX 78476
(512) 888-3331

Suite 114
4300 Amon Canter Blvd.
Fort Worth, TX 76155
(817) 885-6500

Room 8A-27
819 Taylor St.
Fort Worth, TX 76102
(817) 334-3777

Suite 320
10737 Gateway W.
El Paso, TX 79935
(915) 540-5676

9301 SW Freeway Suite 550
Houston, TX 77074-1591
(713) 773-6500

Room 500
222 East Van Buren Street
Harlingen, TX 78550
(512) 427-8533

Room 200
1611 Tenth Street
Lubbock, TX 79401
(806) 743-7462

Room 103
505 E. Travis
Marshall, TX 75670
(903) 935-5257

Suite 200
7400 Blanco Road
San Antonio, TX 78216
(512) 229-4535

Utah
Room 2237
Federal Building
125 South State Street
Salt Lake City, UT 84138-1195
(801) 524-5800

Virginia
Room 3015
400 N. 8th Street
Richmond, VA 23240
(804) 771-2400

Virgin Islands
Suite 7
4200 United Shopping Plaza
St. Croix, VI 00820
(809) 778-5380

Room 210
Veterans Drive
St. Thomas, VI 00802
(809) 774-8530

Vermont
Room 205
87 State Street
Montpelier, VT 05602
(802) 828-4422

Washington
Room 1792
915 Second Avenue
Seattle, WA 98174-1088
(206) 553-1420

Wisconsin
Room 213
212 E. Washington Avenue
Madison, WI 53703
(608) 264-5261

Suite 400
310 W. Wisconsin Avenue
Milwaukee, WI 53203
(414) 297-3941

West Virginia
Room 309
550 Eagan Street
Charleston, WV 25301
(304) 347-5220

5th Floor
168 W. Main Street
Clarksburg, WV 26301
(304) 623-5631

Wyoming
Room 4001
Federal Building
100 East B Street
999 18th Street
Casper, WY 82602-2839
(307) 261-5761

SBA FIELD OFFICES
REGIONAL OFFICES

REGION I
155 Federal St.
Ninth Floor
Boston, MA 02110
(617) 451-2023

REGION II
26 Federal Plaza
Room 31-08
New York, NY 10278
(212) 264-1450

REGION III
475 Allendale Road
Suite 201
King of Prussia, PA 19406
(215) 962-3700

REGION IV
1375 Peachtree St., N.E.
Fifth Floor
Atlanta, GA 30367-8102
(404) 347-2797

REGION V
300 S. Riverside Plaza
Suite 1975 S
Chicago, IL 60606-6617
(312) 353-5000

REGION VI
8625 King George Drive
Building C
Dallas, TX 75235-3391
(214) 767-7633

REGION VII
911 Walnut St.
13th Floor
Kansas City, MO 64106
(816) 426-3608

REGION VIII
999 18th St.
Suite 701
Denver, CO 80202
(303) 294-7186

REGION IX
71 Stevenson St.
20th Floor
San Francisco, CA 94105-2939
(415) 744-6402

REGION X
2615 Fourth Ave.
Room 440
Seattle, WA 98121
(206) 553-5676

Appendix 3

U.S. Department of Commerce

Country Desk Officers

Note: Persons designed EEBIC are affiliated with the Eastern Europe Business Information Center.

The area code for telephoning these desk officers long distance is 202. Letters should be addressed to the individual at his or her room number, U.S. Department of Commerce, Washington, DC, 20230.

COUNTRY	DESK OFFICER	PHONE (202)	ROOM NO.
Afghanistan	Stanislaw Bilinski	377-2954	2029B
Albania	Elizabeth Brown/EEBIC	377-2645	6403
Algeria	Jeffrey Johnson	377-4652	2039
Angola	Stephen Lamar	377-5148	3317
Argentina	Randy Mye	377-1548	3021
Arbua	Thomas Wilde	377-2527	3020
ASEAN	George Paine	377-3875	CALL

COUNTRY	DESK OFFICER	PHONE (202)	ROOM NO.
Australia	Karen Wilde (Policy)	377-3646	2308
	Gary Bouck (Business)	377-2920	3415
Bahamas	Americo A. Tadeu	377-2527	3020
Bahrain	Claude Clement	377-5545	2039
Bangladesh	Stanlislaw Bilinski	377-2954	2029B
Barbados	Thomas Wilde	377-2527	3020
Belgium	Boyce Fitzpatrick	377-5401	3415
Belize	Americo Tadeu	377-2527	3020
Benin	Reginald Biddle	377-4388	3317
Bermuda	Thomas Wilde	377-2527	3020
Bhutan	Stanislaw Bilinski	377-2954	2029B
Bolivia	Laura Zeiger	377-2521	3029
Botswana	Stephen Lamar	377-5148	3317
Brazil	Roger Turner/Larry Farris	377-3871	3017
Brunei	Vacant	377-3875	2034
Bulgaria	Elizabeth Brown/EEBIC	377-2645	6043
Burkina Faso	Philip Michelini	377-4388	3317
Burma	Jean Kelly	377-3875	2034
Burundi	Vacant	377-0357	3317
Cambodia	Kent Stouffer	377-3875	2308
Cameroon	Vacant	377-0357	3317
Canada	Kenneth Fernandez /Stephen Jacobs /William Cavitt	377-0357	3033
Cape Verde	Philip Michelini	377-4368	3317
Caymans	Randy Mye	377-2527	3020
Central Africa Republic	Vacant	377-0357	3317
Chad	Vacant	377-0357	3317
Chile	Mark Siegelman	377-1495	3021
Colombia	Laurie MacNamara	377-1659	3025
CIS (formerly USSR)	Susan Lewengl/ Leslie Brown	377-4655	3414
Comoros	Vacant	377-4564	3317
Congo	Vacant	377-0357	3317
Costa Rica	Julie Rauner	377-2527	3020
Cuba	Kathleen Scanlan	377-2527	3020
Cyprus	Ann Corro	377-3945	3044

COUNTRY	DESK OFFICER	PHONE (202)	ROOM NO.
Czechoslovakia	Shelley Galbraith/EEBBIC	377-2645	6043
Denmark	Maryanne Lyons	377-3254	3413
Djibouti	Vacant	377-4564	3317
Dominica	Vacant	377-2527	3020
Dominican Republic	Thomas Welch	377-2527	3020
East Caribbean	Thomas Wilde	377-2527	3020
Ecuador	Laurie MacNamara	377-1659	3025
Egypt	Thomas Sams	377-4441	2039
El Salvador	Paul Moore	377-2527	3020
Equatorial Guinea	Vacant	377-0357	3317
Ethiopia	Vacant	377-4564	3317
European Community	Charles Ludolph	377-5276	3036
Finland	Maryanne Lyons	377-3254	3413
France	Maria Aronson/ Kelly Jacobs	377-8008	3042
French Antilles	Thomas Welch	377-2527	3020
French Guiana	Thomas Welch	377-2527	3020
Gabon	Vacant	377-0357	3317
Gambia	Reginald Biddle	377-4388	3317
Germany	Shell Galbraith/EEBIC/	377-2645	6043
	Velizar Stanoyevitch	377-2434	3411
Ghana	Reginald Biddle	377-4388	3317
Greece	Ann Corro	377-3945	3044
Grenada	Thomas Wilde	377-2527	3020
Guadeloupe	Thomas Welch	377-2527	3314
Guatemala	America A. Tadeu	377-2527	3020
Guinea	Philip Michelini	377-4388	3317
Guinea-Bissau	Philip Michelini	377-4388	3317
Guyana	Thomas Welch	377-2527	3020
Haiti	Thomas Welch	377-2527	3020
Honduras	Paul Moore	377-2527	3020
Hong Kong	Jenelle Matheson/ Jeffrey Bynum	377-3583	2317
Hungary	Russell Johnson/EEBIC	377-2645	6043
Iceland	Maryanne Lyons	377-3254	3413
India	John Simmons/John Crown Tim Gilman	377-2954	2029B
Indonesia	Karen Wilde	377-3875	2034

COUNTRY	DESK OFFICER	PHONE (202)	ROOM NO.
Iran	Claude Clement	377-5545	2039
Iraq	Thomas Sams	377-4441	2039
Ireland	Brenda Fisher	377-4104	3049
Israel	Kate Fitzgerald-Wilks		
	Doris Nelmas	377-4652	2039
Italy	Noel Negretti	377-2177	3045
Ivory Coast	Philip Michelini	377-4388	3317
Jamaica	Thomas Wilde	377-2527	3020
Japan	Ed Leslie	377-4527	2318
Jordan	Corey Wright	377-2515	2039
Kampuchea	Kent Stouffer	377-3875	2308
Kenya	Vacant	377-4564	3317
Korea (North)	JeNelle Matheson/		
	Jeff Bynum	377-3583	2317
Korea (South)	Karen Chopra/	377-4399	2329
	Ian Davis/Dan Duvall	377-4390	2329
Kuwait	Corey Wright	377-2515	2039
Laos	Kent Stouffer	377-3875	2308
Lebanon	Corey Wright	377-2515	2039
Lesotho	Stephan Lamar	377-5148	3317
Liberia	Reginald Biddle	377-4388	3317
Libya	Claude Clement	377-5545	2039
Luxembourg	Boyce Fitzpatrick	377-5401	3415
Macao	JeNelle Matheson/		
	Jeff Bynum	377-3583	2317
Madagascar	Vacant	377-2564	3317
Malawi	Stephen Lamar	377-5148	3317
Malaysia	Allison Lester	377-3875	2034
Maldives	Stanislaw Bilinski	377-2954	2029B
Mali	Philip Michelini	377-4388	3317
Malta	Robert McLaughlin	377-3748	3049
Martinique	Americo A. Tadeu	377-2527	3020
Mauritania	Philip Michelini	377-4564	3317
Mauritius	Vacant	377-4564	3317
Mexico	Ted Johnson/		
	Andrew Lowry		
	Elise Pinkow	377-4464	3028
Mongolia	JeNelle Matheson/		
	Jeff Bynum	377-3583	2317
Morocco	Claude Clement	377-5545	2039
Mozambique	Stephen Lamar	377-5148	3317

COUNTRY	DESK OFFICER	PHONE (202)	ROOM NO.
Namibia	Emily Solomon	377-5148	3317
Nepal	Stanislaw Bilinski	377-2954	2029B
Netherlands	Boyce Fitzpatrick	377-5401	3415
Netherlands Antilles	Thomas Wilde	377-2527	3020
New Zealand	Gary Brouck (Business)/	377-3646	2308
	Karen Wilde (Policy)	377-3646	2308
Nicaragua	Julie Rauner	377-2527	3020
Niger	Philip Michelini	377-4388	3317
Nigeria	Reginald Biddle	377-4388	3317
Norway	James Devlin	377-4414	3413
Oman	Claude Clement	377-5545	2039
Pacific Islands	Gary Bouck/Karen Wilde	377-3646	2308
Pakistan	Cheryl McQueen	377-2954	2029B
Panama	Julie Rauner	377-2527	3020
Paraguay	Randy Mye	377-1548	3021
People's Rep. of China	Christine Lucyk	377-5527	2317
Peru	Laura Zeiger	377-2521	3029
Philippines	George Paine	377-3875	2034
Poland	Michael Arsenault		
	Mary Moskaluk/EEBIC	377-2645	6043
Portugal	Ann Corro	377-3954	3044
Puerto Rico	Thomas Welch	377-2527	3020
Qatar	Claude Clement	377-5545	2039
Romania	Elizabeth Brown/EEBIC	377-2645	6043
Rwanda	Vacant	377-0357	3317
San Tome & Principe	Vacant	377-0357	3317
Saudi Arabia	Jeffrey Johnson	377-4652	2039
Senegal	Philip Michelini	377-4388	3317
Seychelles	Vacant	377-4564	3317
Sierra Leone	Reginald Biddle	377-4388	3317
Singapore	Allison Lester	377-3875	2034
Somalia	Vacant	377-4564	3317
South Africa	Emily Solomon	377-5148	3317
Spain	Richard Humbert	377-4508	3042
Sri Lanka	Stanislaw Bilinski	377-2954	2029B
St. Bathelemey	Americo A. Tadeu	377-2527	3314
St. Kitts-Nevis	Thomas Wilde	377-2527	3314
St. Lucia	Thomas Wilde	377-2527	3314

COUNTRY	DESK OFFICER	PHONE (202)	ROOM NO.
St. Maarten	Thomas Welch	377-2527	3314
St. Vincent- Grenadines	Tom Klotzbach	377-2527	3314
Sudan	Vacant	377-4564	3317
Suriname	Thomas Welch	377-2527	3020
Swaziland	Stephen Lamar	377-5148	3317
Sweden	James Devlin	377-4414	3413
Switzerland	Philip Combs	377-2920	3415
Syria	Corey Wright	377-2515	2039
Taiwan	Laura Scogna/Dan Duvall	377-4390	2329
Tanzania	Stephen Lamar	377-5148	3317
Thailand	Jean Kelly	377-3875	2034
Togo	Reginald Biddle	377-4564	3317
Trinidad & Tobago	Thomas Wilde	377-2527	3020
Tunisia	Corey Wright	377-2515	2039
Turkey	Geoffrey Jackson	377-3945	3042
Turks & Caicos Islands	Americo A. Tadeu	377-2527	3020
Uganda	Vacant	377-4564	3317
United Arab Emirates	Claude Clement	377-5545	2039
United Kingdom	Robert McLaughlin	377-3748	3045
Uruguay	Mark Siegelman	377-1495	3021
USSR (CIS)	Susan Lewenz/Leslie Brown	377-4655	3414
Venezuela	Herbert Lindow	377-4303	3029
Vietnam	Kent Stouffer	377-3875	2308
Virgin Islands (UK)	Thomas Wilde	377-2527	3020
Virgin Islands (U.S.)	Thomas Welch	377-2527	3020
Yemen, Republic of	Corey Wright	377-2515	2039
Yugoslavia	Jeremy Keller	377-5373	3046
Zaire	Vacant	377-0357	3317
Zambia	Stephen Lamar	377-5148	3317
Zimbabwe	Stephen Lamar	377-5148	3317

Appendix 4

International Trade Administration U.S. and Foreign Commercial Service

Susan C. Schwab
Assistant Secretary and Director General
U.S. and Foreign Commercial Service
Room 3802, HCH Building
14th & Constitution Avenue, NW
Washington, DC 20230
(202) 377-5777
FTS 377-5777

Joseph A. Vasquez, Jr.
Principal Deputy Assistant Secretary
U.S. and Foreign Commercial Service
Room 3802, HCH Building
14th & Constitution Avenue, NW
Washington, DC 20230
(202) 377-0725
FTS 377-0725

Daniel E. Sullivan
Deputy Assistant Secretary for Domestic Operations
U.S. and Foreign Commercial Service
Room 3802, HCH Building

14th & Constitution Avenue, NW
Washington, DC 20230
(202) 377-5777, FAX 377-0687
FTS 377-4767

Alabama

Birmingham - Gayly C. Shelton, Jr., Director
Room 302 Berry Building
2015 2nd Avenue North, 35203
(206) 731-1331, FAX 731-0076, FTS 229-1331

Alaska

Anchorage-Charles Becker
Suite 319 World Trade Center Alaska
4201 Tudor Center Dr., 99508
(907) 271-6237, FAX 271-6242, FTS 868-6237

Arizona

Phoenix - Donald W. Fry, Director
Room 3412 Federal Building
230 North 1st Avenue, 85025
(602) 379-3285, FAX 379-4324, FTS 261-3285

Arkansas

Little Rock - Lon J. Hardin, Director
Suite 811 Savers Federal Building
320 West Capitol Avenue, 72201
(501) 324-5794, FAX 324-7380, FTS 740-5794

California

Los Angeles - Stephen Arlinghaus, Director
Room 9200
11000 Wilshire Blvd., 90024
(213) 575-7104,FAX 575-7220, FTS 793-7104

Santa Ana
Suite #1
116-A West 4th Street 92701
(714) 836-2461,FAX 836-2332, FTS 799-2461

San Diego - Richard Powell, Director
Suite 145
6363 Greenwich Drive, 92122
(619) 557-5395, FAX 557-6176, FTS 895-5395

San Francisco - Betty D. Neuhart, Director
14th Floor
250 Montgomery Street, 94104
District Office: (415) 705-2300, FTS 465-2300
Regional Office: (415) 705-2310, FTS 465-2310
FAX: (415) 705-2299

Colorado

Denver - Nell Hesse, Director
Suite 680
1625 Broadway, 80202
(303) 844-3246, FAX 844-5651, FTS 564-3246

Connecticut

Hartford - Eric B. Outwater, Director
Room 610B Federal Building
450 Main Street, 06103
(203) 240-3530, FAX 240-3473, FTS 244-3530

Delaware

Served by Philadelphia District Office

Florida

Miami - Ivan A. Cosimi, Director
Suite 224 Federal Building
51 S. W. First Avenue, 33130
(305) 536-5257, FAX 536-4765, FTS 350-5267

Clearwater
128 North Osceola Avenue, 34615
(813) 461-0011, FAX 449-2889, FTS 826-3738

Orlando
C/O Central Florida University
College of Business Administration
Room 346 CEBA II, 32816
(407) 648-6235, FTS 820-6235

Tallahassee
Room 401 Collins Bldg
107 West Gaines Street, 32304
(904) 488-6469,FAX 487-1407, FTS 965-9635

Georgia

Atlanta - George T. Norton, Director
Plaza Square North
4360 Chamblee-Dunwoody Rd., 30341
(404) 452-9101, FAX 452-9105, FTS None

Savannah - Barbara Prieto, Trade Spec.-in-Charge
Room A-107
120 Barnard Street, 31401
(912) 944-4204, FAX 944-4241, FTS 248-4204

Hawaii

Honolulu - George B. Dolan, Director
P.O. Box 50026
400 Ala Moana Blvd, 96850
(808) 541-1782,FAX 541-3435, FTS 551-1782

Idaho

Boise - Portland, Oregon District
2nd Floor Joe R. Williams Building
700 West State Street, 83720
(208) 334-3857, FAX 334-2631, FTS 554-9254

Illinois

Chicago - LoRee P. Silloway, Director
Room 1406
55 East Monroe Street, 60603
(312) 353-4450, FAX 886-8025, FTS 353-4450

Wheaton - Illinois Institute of Technology
201 East Loop Road, 60187
(312) 353-4332, FAX 353-4336, FTS 353-4332

Rockford
P.O. Box 1747
515 North Court Street, 61110-0247
(815) 987-8123, FAX 987-8122, FTS 363-4347

Indiana

Indianapolis - Andrew W. Thress, Director
Suite 520
One North Capitol, 46204
(317) 226-6214, FAX 226-6139, FTS 331-6214

Iowa

Des Moines - John H. Steuber, Jr., Director
Room 817 Federal Building
210 Walnut Street, 50309
(515) 284-4222, FAX 284-4021, FTS 862-4222

Cedar Rapids
424 First Avenue NE 52401
(319) 362-8418, FAX 398-5228, FTS None

Kansas

Wichita - Kansas City, Missouri District
151 N. Valutsia, 67214-4695
(316) 269-6160, FAX 683-7326, FTS 752-6160

Kentucky

Louisville - John Autin, director
Room. 636B
Gene Snyder Courthouse and Customhouse Bldg.
601 West Broadway, 40202
(502) 582-5066, FAX 582-6573, FTS 352-5066

Louisiana

New Orleans - Paul L. Guldry, Director
432 World Trade Center
#2 Canal Street, 70130
(504) 589-6546, FAX 589-2337, FTS 682-6546

Maine

Augusta - Boston District Office
77 Sewall Street, 04330
(207) 622-8249, FAX 626-9156, FTS 833-6249

Maryland

Baltimore - David Earle, Director
413 U.S. Customhouse
40 South Gay Street, 21202
(301) 962-3560, FAX 962-7813, FTS 922-3560

Gaithersburg
c/o National Institute of Standards & Technology
Building 411, 20899
(301) 962-3560, FAX 962-7813, FTS 922-3560

Massachusetts

Boston - Francis J. O'Conner, Director
Suite 307 World Trade Center
Commonwealth Pier Area, 02210
(617) 565-8563, FAX 565-8530, FTS 922-8563

Michigan

Detroit - Vacant, Director
1140 McNamara Building
477 Michigan Avenue, 48226
(313) 226-3650, FAX 226-3657, FTS 226-835-8563

Grand Rapids
300 Monroe NW, 49503
(616) 456-2411, FAX 456-3657, FTS 835-8563

Minnesota

Minneapolis - Ronald E. Kramer, Director
108 Federal Building
110 South 4th Street, 55401
(612) 346-1638, FAX 348-1650, FTS 777-1638

Mississippi

Jackson - Mark E. Spinney, Director
328 Jackson Mall Office Center
300 Woodrow Wilson Blvd., 39213
(601) 965-4388, FAX 965-5386, FTS 490-4388

Missouri

St. Louis - Donald R. Loso, Director
Suite 610
7911 Forsyth Blvd., 63105
(314) 425-3302, FAX 425-3381, FTS 279-3302

Kansas City - John R. Kupfer, Director
Room 635
601 East 12th Street, 64106
(816) 426-3141, FAX 426-3140, FTS 867-3141

Montana

Served by the Portland District Office

Nebraska

Omaha - George H. Payne, Director
11133 "O" Street, 68137
(402) 221-3664, FAX 221-3668, FTS 864-3664

Nevada

Reno - Joseph J. Jeremy, Director
1755 East Plumb Lane, #152, 89502
(702) 784-5203, FAX 784-5343, FTS 470-5203

New Hampshire

Served by the Boston District Office

New Jersey

Trenton - Thomas J. Murray, Director
Suite 100
3131 Princeton Pike Bldg. #6, 08648
(609) 989-2100,FAX 989-2395, FTS 483-2100

New Mexico

Albuquerque - Dallas District Office
3rd Floor
625 Silver SW, 87102
(505) 766-2070, FAX 766-1057, FTS 474-2070

New York

Buffalo - George Buchanan, Director
1312 Federal Building
111 West Huron Street, 14202
(716) 846-4191, FAX 8460-5290, FTS 437-4191

Rochester
Suite 20
111 East Avenue, 14604
(716) 263-6480, FAX 325-6505, FTS 963-6480

New York - Joel W. Barkan, Director
Room 3718
26 Federal Plaza, 10278
(212) 264-0600, FAX 264-1356, FTS 264-0600

North Carolina

Greensboro - Samuel P. Troy, Director
Room 203
324 West Market Street
P.O. Box 1950, 27402
(919) 333-4345, FAX 333-5158, FTS 699-5345

North Dakota

Serviced by the Omaha District Office

Ohio

Cincinnati - Gordon B. Thomas, Director
9504 Federal Building
550 Main Street, 45202
(513) 684-2944, FAX 684-3200, FTS 684-2944

Cleveland - Toby T. Zettler, Director
Room 600
668 Euclid Avenue, 44114
(216) 622-4750, FAX 522-2235, FTS 942-4750

Oklahoma

Oklahoma City - Ronald L. Wilson, Director
6601 Broadway Extension, 73116
(405) 231-5302, FAX 841-5245, FTS 736-5302

Tulsa
440 South Houston Street, 74127
(918) 581-7650, FAX 581-2844, FTS 745-7650

Oregon

Portland - William Schrage, Director
Suite 242 One World Trade Center
121 SW Salmon, 97204
(503) 326-3001, FAX 326-6351, FTS 423-3001

Pennsylvania

Philadelphia - Robert E. Kistler, Director
Suite 202
475 Allendale Road
King of Prussia, 19406
(215) 962-4980, FAX 951-7959, FTS 486-7954

Pittsburgh - John A. McCartney, Director
2002 Federal Building
1000 Liberty Avenue, 15222
(412) 644-2850, FAX 644-4875, FTS 722-2850

Puerto Rico

San Juan (Hato Rey) - J. Enrique Vilella, Director
Room G-55 Federal Building
Chardon Avenue, 00918
(809) 766-5555, FAX 766-5692, FTS 498-5555

Rhode Island

Providence - Boston District Office
7 Jackson Walkway, 02903
(401) 528-5104, FAX 528-5067, FTS 838-5104

South Carolina

Columbia - Edgar L. Rojas, Director
Suite 172
Strom Thurmond Federal Building
1835 Assembly Street, 29201
(803) 765-5345, FAX 253-3614, FTS 677-5345

Charleston
Room 128
J.C. Long Building
9 Liberty Street, 29424
(803) 724-4361, FTS 677-4361

South Dakota

Served by the Omaha District Office

Tennessee

Nashville - Jim Charlet, Director
Suite 1114
Parkway Towers
404 James Robertson Parkway, 37219-1505
(615) 736-5161, FAX 736-2454, FTS 852-5161

Memphis
Suite 200
Falls Building
22 North Front Street, 38103
(901) 544-4137, FTS 222-4137

Knoxville
301 East Church Avenue, 37915
(615) 549-9268, FTS 854-9268

Texas

Dallas - Donald Schilke, Director
Room 7A5
1100 Commerce Street, 75242-0787
(214) 767-0542, FAX 767-8240, FTS 729-0542

Austin
Suite 1200
816 Congress Avenue
P.O. Box 12728, 78711
(512) 482-5939, FAX 320-9674, FTS 770-5939

Houston - James D. Cook, Director
Room 2625 Federal Courthouse Building
515 Rusk Street, 77002
(713) 229-2578, FAX 229-2203, FTS 526-4578

Utah

Salt Lake City - Stephen P. Smoot, Director
Suite 105
324 South State Street, 84111
(801) 524-5116, FAX 524-5886, FTS 588-5116

Vermont

Served by the Boston District Office

Virginia

Richmond - Philip A. Ouzts, Director
8010 Federal Building
400 North 8th Street, 23240
(804) 771-2246, FAX 771-2390, FTS 925-2246

Washington

Seattle - Charles Buck, Director
Suite 290
3131 Elliott Avenue, 98121
(206) 553-5615, FAX 553-7253, FTS 925-2246

Spokane
Room 625
West 806 Spokane Falls Blvd., 99201
(509) 353-2922, FAX 625-6188, FTS 439-2922

West Virginia

Charleston - Roger Fortner, Director
Suite 609
405 Capitol Street, 25301
(304) 347-5123, FAX 347-5408, FTS 930-5123

Wisconsin

Milwaukee - Johnny Brown, Director
Room 596
517 East Wisconsin Avenue, 53202
(414) 297-3473, FAX 297-3470, FTS 362-3473

Wyoming

Served by the Denver District Office

Appendix 5

Small Business Development Centers

SBDCs are supported by SBA annually in 49 states for $50 million. SBDC's offer "one stop" assistance to small businesses, making a variety of information and guidance available on management techniques and technology. Most SBDCs are headquartered at one of the 56 "lead" universities or colleges with nearly 600 subcenters located through the U.S. in easily accessible locations.

ALABAMA

Ms. Pat Thompson
Acting State Director
Small Business Development Center
University of Alabama in Birmingham
17178 11th Avenue South, Suite 419
Birmingham, AL 35294
(205) 934-7260
(205) 934-7645 FAX

ALASKA

Ms. Jan Fredericks
State Director

Small Business Development Center
University of Alaska/Anchorage
430 West 7th Avenue, Suite 115
Anchorage, AK 99501
(907) 274-7232
(907) 274-9524 FAX

ARIZONA

Mr. Dave Smith
State Director
Small Business Development Center
Gateway Community College
108 North 40th Street, Suite 148
Phoenix, AZ 85034
(602) 392-5224
(602) 392-5300 FAX

ARKANSAS

Mr. Paul McGinnis
State Director
Small Business Development Center
University of Arkansas
Little Rock Technology Center
100 South Main, Suite 401
Little Rock, AR 72201
(501) 324-9043
(501) 324-9049 FAX

CALIFORNIA

Dr. Edward Kawahara
State Director
Small Business Development Center
Department of Commerce
801 K Street, Suite 1600
Sacramento, CA 95814
(916) 324-9234

COLORADO

Mr. Rick Garcia
State Director
Small Business Development Center
Office of Business Development
1625 Broadway, Suite 1710
Denver, CO 80203
(303) 892-3840
(303) 892-3848 FAX

CONNECTICUT

Mr. John P. O'Conner
State Director
Small Business Development Center
University of Connecticut
Box U-41, Room. 422
368 Fairfield Road
Storrs, CT 06268
(203) 486-4135
(203) 486-1576 FAX

DELAWARE

Ms. Linda Fayerweather
State Director
Small Business Development Center
University of Delaware
Suite 005 - Purnell Hall
Newark, DE 19711
(302) 451-2747
(302) 451-6750 FAX

DISTRICT OF COLUMBIA

Ms. Nancy A. Flake
State Director
Small Business Development Center
Howard University
2600 6th Street, NW
Washington, DC 20059
(202) 806-1550
(202) 806-1777 FAX

FLORIDA

Mr. Jerry Cartwright
State. Director
Small Business Development Center
University of West Florida
11000 University Parkway
Pensacola, FL 32514
(904) 474-3016
(904) 474-2030 FAX

GEORGIA

Mr. Hank Logan
State Director
Small Business Development Center

University of Georgia
Chicopee Complex
Athens, GA 30602
(404) 542-5760
(404) 542-6776 FAX

HAWAII

Ms. Janet Nye
State Director
Small Business Development Center
University of Hawaii at Hilo
523 West Lanikaula Street
Hilo, HI 96720-4091
(808) 933-3515
(808) 933-3622 FAX

IDAHO

Mr. Ronald R. Hall
State Director
Small Business Development Center
Boise State University
College of Business
1910 University Drive
Boise, ID 83725
(208) 385-1640
(208) 385-3877 FAX

ILLINOIS

Mr. Jeffrey J. Mitchell
State Director
Small Business Development Center
Department of Commerce and Community Affairs
620 East Adams Street
Springfield, IL 62701
(217) 524-5856
(217) 785-6328 FAX

INDIANA

Mr. Steve Thrash
State Director
Small Business Development Center
Economic Development Council
One North Capitol, Suite 420
Indianapolis, IN 46204-2248
(317) 264-6871
(317) 264-3102 FAX

IOWA

Mr. Ronald Manning
State Director
Small Business Development Center
Iowa State University
137 Lynn Avenue
Ames, IA 50010
(515) 292-6351
(515) 292-0020 FAX

KANSAS

Mr. Tom Hull
State Director
Small Business Development Center
Wichita State University
Campus Box 148
Wichita, KS 67208-1595
(316) 689-3193
(316) 689-3647 FAX

KENTUCKY

Ms. Janet Holloway
State Director
Small Business Development Center
University of Kentucky
College of Business and Economics
205 Business & Economics Building
Lexington, KY 40506-00341
(606) 257-7668
(606) 258-1907 FAX

LOUISIANA

Dr. John Baker
State Director
Small Business Development Center
Northeast Louisiana University
College of Business Administration
700 University Avenue
Monroe, LA 71209
(318) 342-5506
(318) 342-5510 FAX

MAINE

Ms. Diane Branscomb
Acting State Director

Small Business Development Center
University of Southern Maine
15 Surrenden Street
Portland, ME 04101
(207) 780-4420
(207) 780-4417 FAX

MARYLAND

Mr. Michael E. Long, Jr.
Acting State Director
Small Business Development Center
Department of Economic and Employment Development
217 East Redwood Street, 10th Floor
Baltimore, MD 21202
(301) 333-6996
(301) 333-6608 FAX

MASSACHUSETTS

Mr. John Ciccarelli
State Director
Small Business Development Center
University of Massachusetts
School of Management
Amherst, MA 01003
(413) 545-6301
(413) 545-1273 FAX

MICHIGAN

Dr. Norman Schlafmann
State Director
Small Business Development Center
Wayne State University
2727 Second Avenue
Detroit, MI 48201
(313) 577-4848
(313) 577-4222 FAX

MINNESOTA

Randall Olson
State Director
Small Business Development Center
Department of Trade and Economic Development
American Center Building
150 East Kellogg Boulevard

St. Paul, MN 55101-1421
(612) 297-5773
(612) 296-1290 FAX

MISSISSIPPI

Mr. Raleigh Byars
State Director
Small Business Development Center
University of Mississippi
Old Chemistry Building, Suite 216
University, MS 38677
(601) 232-5001
(601) 232-7010 FAX

MISSOURI

Mr. Max E. Summers
State Director
Small Business Development Center
University of Missouri
Suite 300, University Place
Columbia, MO 65211
(314) 882-1348
(314) 884-4297 FAX

MONTANA

Mr. Evan McKinney
Acting State Director
Small Business Development Center
Department of Commerce
1424 Ninth Avenue
Helena, MT 59620
(406) 444-4780
(406) 444-2808 FAX

NEBRASKA

Mr. Robert Bernie
State Director
Small Business Development Center
University of Nebraska at Omaha
Peter Kiewit Center
Omaha, NE 68182
(402) 554-2521
(402) 595-2388 FAX

NEVADA

Mr. Samuel Males
State Director
Small Business Development Center
University of Nevada in Reno
College of Business Administration, Room 411
Reno, NV 89557-0016
(702) 784-1717
(702) 784-4305 FAX

NEW HAMPSHIRE

Ms. Helen Goodman
State Director
Small Business Development Center
University of New Hampshire
108 McConnell Hall
Durham, NH 03824
(603) 862-2200
(603) 862-4468 FAX

NEW JERSEY

Ms. Brenda B. Hopper
State Director
Small Business Development Center
Rutgers University
Ackerson Hall - 3rd Floor
180 University Street
Newark, NJ 07102
(201) 648-5950
(201) 648-1110 FAX

NEW MEXICO

Mr. Randy Grissom
State Director
Small Business Development Center
Santa Fe Community College
P.O. Box 4187
Santa Fe, NM 87502-4187
(505) 438-1237 FAX

NEW Y0RK

Mr. James L. King
State Director
Small Business Development Center
State University of New York

SUNY Upstate
SUNY Plaza, S-523
Albany, NY 12246
(518) 443-5398
(518) 465-4992 FAX

Dr. Solomon S. Kabuka, Jr.
Director
Small Business Development Center
University of The Virgin Islands
Grand Hotel Building, Annex B
P.O. Box 1087
St. Thomas, U.S. Virgin Islands 00804
(809) 776-3206
(809) 775-3756 FAX

NORTH CAROLINA

Mr. Scott Daugherty
State Director
Small Business Development Center
University of North Carolina
4509 Creedmoor Road, Suite 201
Raleigh, NC 27612
(919) 571-4154
(919) 787-9284 FAX

NORTH DAKOTA

Mr. Wally Kearns
State Director
Small Business Development Center
University of North Dakota
Gamble Hall, University Station
Grand Forks, ND 58202-7308
(701) 777-3700
(701) 223-3081 FAX

OHIO

Mr. Jack Brown
State Director
Small Business Development Center
Department of Development
30 East Broad Street
Columbus, OH 43266-1001
(614) 466-5111

OKLAHOMA

Dr. Grady Pennington
State Director
Small Business Development Center
Southeast Oklahoma State University
517 West University
Station A, Box 2584
Durant, OK 74701
(405) 924-0277
(405) 924-8531 FAX

OREGON

Mr. Sandy Cutler
State Director
Small Business Development Center
Lane Community College
99 West 10th Avenue, Suite 216
Eugene, OR 97401
(503) 726-2250
(503) 345-6006 FAX

PENNSYLVANIA

Mr. Gregory L. Higgins
State Director
Small Business Development Center
University of Pennsylvania
The Wharton School
444 Vance Hall
Philadelphia, PA 19104
(215) 898-1219
(215) 898-1299 FAX

PUERTO RICO

Mr. Jose M. Romaguera
Director
Small Business Development Center
University of Puerto Rico
Box 5253 - College Station
Building B
Mayaguez, PR 00708
(809) 834-3590 or 834-3790

RHODE ISLAND

Mr. Douglas Jobling
State Director

Small Business Development Center
Bryant College
1150 Douglas Pike
Smithfield, RI 02917-1284
(401) 232-6111
(401) 232-6319 FAX

SOUTH CAROLINA

Mr. John Lenti
State Director
Small Business Development Center
University of South Carolina
College of Business Administration
1710 College Street
Columbia, SC 29208
(803) 777-4907
(803) 777-4403 FAX

SOUTH DAKOTA

M. Donald Greenfield
State Director
Small Business Development Center
University of South Dakota
School of Business
414 East Clark
Vermilion, SD 57069
(605) 677-5272
(605) 677-5427 FAX

TENNESSEE

Dr. Kenneth J. Burns
State Director
Small Business Development Center
Memphis State University
Memphis, TN 38152
(901) 678-2500
(901) 678-4072 FAX

TEXAS

Dr. Elizabeth Gatewood
Region Director
Small Business Development Center
University of Houston
601 Jefferson, Suite 2330

Houston, TX 77002
(713) 752-8444
(713) 752-8484 FAX

Mr. Robert M. McKinley
Region Director
South Texas-Border
Small Business Development Center
University of Texas at San Antonio
San Antonio, TX 78285-0660
(512) 224-0791
(512) 222-9834 FAX

Mr. Craig Bean
Acting Region Director
Northwest Texas
Small Business Development Center
Texas Tech University
2579 South Loop 289, Suite 114
Lubbock, TX 79423-1637
(806) 745-3973
(806) 745-6207 FAX

Ms. Marty Jones
Region Director
North Texas
Small Business Development Center
Dallas Community College
1402 Corinth Street
Dallas, TX 75215
(214) 565-5831
(214) 324-7945 FAX

UTAH

Mr. David Nimkin
State Director
Small Business Development Center
University of Utah
102 West 500 South
Salt Lake City, UT 84102
(801) 581-7905
(801) 581-7814 FAX

VERMONT

Mr. Norris Elliott
State Director
Small Business Development Center

THE BUSINESS BOOKSHELF

These books have been carefully selected as the best on these subjects. Your satisfaction is guaranteed or your money back.

To order, call toll-free (800) 255-5730 extension 110. Please have your Visa, Mastercard, American Express or Discover card ready.

Money Sources for Small Business
How You Can Find Private, State, Federal, and Corporate Financing
By William Alarid. Many potential successful business owners simply don't have enough cash to get started. *Money Sources* shows how to get money from Federal, State, Venture Capital Clubs, Corporations, Computerized Matching Services, Small Business Investment Companies plus many other sources. Includes samples of loan applications.
ISBN 0-940673-51-7   224 pages   8 1/2 x 11   paperbound $19.95
See special offer on last page!

Small Time Operator
How to Start Your Own Business, Keep Your Books, Pay Your Taxes, and Stay Out of Trouble
By Bernard Kamaroff, C.P.A. The most popular small business book in the U.S., it's used by over 250,000 businesses. Easy to read and use, *Small Time Operator* is particularly good for those without bookkeeping experience. Comes complete with a year's supply of ledgers and worksheets designed especially for small businesses, and contains invaluable information on permits, licenses, financing, loans, insurance, bank accounts, etc.
ISBN 0-917510-10-0 190 pages 8½x11 paperbound $14.95

Puma Publishing • 1670 Coral Drive, Suite R
Santa Maria, California 93454

The Business Planning Guide
Creating a Plan for Success in Your Own Business
By Andy Bangs. *The Business Planning Guide* has been used by
hundreds of banks, colleges, and accounting firms to guide business
owners through the process of putting together a complete and
effective business plan and financing proposal. The *Guide* comes
complete with examples, forms and worksheets that make the
planning process painless. With over 150,000 copies in print,
the *Guide* has become a small business classic.
ISBN 0-936894-39-3 184 pages 8½x11 paperbound $19.95

Free Help from Uncle Sam to Start Your Own Business
(Or Expand the One You Have) 3rd Edition
By William Alarid and Gustav Berle. *Free Help* describes over 100
government programs that help small business and give dozens of
examples of how others have used this aid. Included are appendices
with helpful books, organizations and phone numbers.
ISBN 0-940673-54-1 304 pages 5½ x 8½ paperbound $13.95

Marketing Without Advertising
By Michael Phillips and Salli Rasberry. A creative and practical guide
that shows small business people how to avoid wasting money on
advertising. The authors, experienced business consultants, show
how to implement an ongoing marketing plan to tell potential and
current customers that yours is a quality business worth trusting,
recommending, and coming back to.
ISBN 0-87337-019-8 200 pages 8½ x 11 paperbound $13.95

Retiring to Your Own Business
*How You Can Launch a Satisfying, Productive and Prosperous
Second Career*
By Gustav Berle. If you're worried about retirement this is the book for
you. In this unique life change book, Gustav Berle gives retired men
and women or those soon to retire a success blueprint. This book
shows how to stay active and involved during your retirement years
while building a richer lifestyle.
ISBN 0-940673-60-6 272 pages 5½ x 8½ paperbound $14.95

Call Toll-Free (800) 255-5730 extension 110.
Please have Visa, Mastercard, American Express or Discover card
ready, or write: Puma Publishing, 1670 Coral Drive, Suite E, Santa
Maria, California 93454.
Sales Tax: Please add 7¾% for shipping to California addresses.
Shipping $2.00 per book; airmail $4.00 per book.

Appendix 6

Government Printing Office Bookstores

A free catalog of all current books, manuals, maps, and artifacts published by the Superintendent of Documents is available from the U. S. Government Printing Office, Washington, DC 20402, phone (202) 783-3238 or from any of the government bookstores. These items may also be purchased with cash or credit card at any of the following locations:

Alabama

O'Neill Building
2021 Third Avenue N
Birmingham, AL 35203
(205) 731-1056

California

ARCO Plaza, C-Level
505 Flower Street
Los Angeles, CA 90071
(213) 894-5841

Room 1023, Federal Building
450 Golden Gate Avenue
San Francisco, CA 94102
(415) 556-0643

Colorado

Room 117, Federal Building
1961 Stout Street
Denver, CO 80294
(303) 844-3964

World Savings Building
720 N. Main Street
Pueblo, CO 81003
(719) 544-3142

District of Colombia

U.S. Government Printing
    Office
710 North Capital Street, NW
Washington, DC 20401
(202) 275-2091

1510 H. Street, NW
Washington, DC 20005
(202) 653-5075

Florida

Room 158, Federal Building
400 W. Bay Street
Jacksonville, FL 32202
(904) 791-3801

Georgia

Room 100, Federal Building
275 Peachtree Street NE
Atlanta, GA 30343
(404) 331-6947

Illinois

Room 1365, Federal Building
219 S. Dearborn Street
Chicago, IL 60604
(312) 353-5133

Maryland

Warehouse Sales Outlet
8660 Cherry Lane
Laurel, MD 20707
(301) 953-7974, 792-0262

Massachusetts

Room 179
Thomas P. O'Neill Building

10 Causeway Street
Boston, MA 02222
(617) 565-6680

Michigan

Suite 160, Federal Building
477 Michigan Avenue
Detroit, MI 48226
(313) 226-7816

Missouri

120 Bannister Mall
5600 E. Bannister Rd.
Kansas City, MO 64137
(816) 765-2256

New York

Room 110
26 Federal Plaza
New York, NY 10278
(212) 264-3825

Ohio

Room 1653, Federal Building
1240 E. 9th Street
Cleveland, OH 44199
(216) 522-4922

Room 207, Federal Building
200 N. High Street
Columbus, OH 43215
(614) 469-6956

Oregon

1305 S.W. First Avenue
Portland, OR 97201-5801
(503) 221-6217

Pennsylvania

Robert Morris Building
100 N. 17th Street
Philadelphia, PA 19103

(215) 597-0677
Room 118, Federal Building
1000 Liberty Avenue
Pittsburgh, PA 15222
(412) 644-2721

Texas

Room 1C46, Federal Building
1100 Commerce Street
Dallas, TX 75242
(214) 767-0076

Suite 12, Texas Crude Building
801 Travis Street
Houston, TX 77002
(713) 653-3100

Washington

Room 194, Federal Building
915 Second Avenue
Seattle, WA 98174
(206) 442-4270

Wisconsin

Room 190, Federal Building
517 E. Wisconsin Avenue
Milwaukee, WI 53202
(414) 297-1304

Appendix 7

General Services Administration Business Service Centers

PHONE: (212) 264-1234
FTS: 264-1234
FAX: 264-2760
MAILING ADDRESS
General Services Administration
Business Service Center
Jacob K. Javits Federal Bldg.
26 Federal Plaza
New York, NY 10278
AREAS SERVICED
New Jersey, New York,
Puerto Rico and Virgin Islands

3ADB
DIRECTOR
John Thompson
Office of Business
and Public Affairs
PHONE: (215) 597-9613
FTS: 597-9613
FAX: 597-1122
MAILING ADDRESS
General Services Administration
Business Service Center
9th & Market Streets
Philadelphia, PA 19107
AREAS SERVICED
Pennsylvania, Delaware, West Virginia
Maryland and Virginia

4ADB
DIRECTOR
Larry Fountain
PHONE: (404) 331-5103
FTS: 841-5103
FAX: 841-5103
MAILING ADDRESS
General Services Administration
Business Service Center
401 West Peachtree Street
Room 2900
Atlanta, GA 30365-2550
AREAS SERVICED
Alabama, Florida, Kentucky,
Georgia, Mississippi, North
Carolina, South Carolina and
Tennessee

5ADB

DIRECTOR
James S. Czysz
PHONE: (312) 353-5383
FTS: 353-5383
FAX: 886-9893
MAILING ADDRESS
General Services Administration
Business Service Center
230 South Dearborn Street
Chicago, IL 60604
AREAS SERVICED
Illinois, Indiana, Ohio,
Michigan, Minnesota and
Wisconsin

6ADB

DIRECTOR
Pat Brown-Dixon
PHONE: (816) 926-7203
FTS: 926-7203
FAX: 926-7513
MAILING ADDRESS
General Services Administration
Business Service Center
1500 East Bannister Road
Kansas City, MO 64131
AREAS SERVICED
Iowa, Kansas, Missouri
and Nebraska

7ADB

DIRECTOR
Dennis C. Armon
PHONE: (817) 334-3284
FTS: 334-3284
FAX: 334-4867
MAILING ADDRESS
General Services Administration
Business Service Center
819 Taylor Street
Fort Worth, TX 76102
AREAS SERVICED
Arkansas, Louisiana,
Texas, New Mexico and
Oklahoma

8ADB-8

DIRECTOR
Darlene Kendrick
PHONE: (303) 236-7408
FTS: 776-7408

FAX: 236-0455
FAX: 776-0455
MAILING ADDRESS
General Services Administration
Business Service Center
B41 Room 141
Denver Federal Center
Denver, CO 80225

AREAS SERVICED
Colorado, North Dakota,
South Dakota, Utah, Wyoming
and Montana

9-ADB-S   DIRECTOR
                 Gerald D. Meckler
                 PHONE: (415) 744-5050
                 FAX: 484-5068
                 MAILING ADDRESS
                 General Services Administration
                 Business Service Center
                 525 Market Street
                 San Francisco, CA 94105
                 AREAS SERVICED
                 Northern California, Hawaii and
                 all of Nevada, except Clark County

9-ADB-L   DIRECTOR
                 Carol Honore
                 PHONE: (213) 894-3210
                 FTS: 798-3210
                 MAILING ADDRESS
                 General Services Administration
                 Business Service Center
                 300 North Los Angeles Street
                 Los Angeles, CA 90012-2000
                 AREAS SERVICED
                 Los Angeles, Southern California,
                 Arizona and Clark County, Nevada

9ADB-10   DIRECTOR
                 Wiletta F. Brown
                 PHONE: (206) 931-7956
                 FTS: 396-7957
                 FAX: 396-7507

                 MAILING ADDRESS
                 General Services Administration

Business Service Center
15th & C Streets, SW
Auburn, WA 98001
AREAS SERVICED
Alaska, Idaho, Oregon
and Washington

WADB

DIRECTOR
Diane Ross
Office of Business
and Public Affairs
PHONE: (202) 708-5804
FAX: 708-6420
MAILING ADDRESS
General Services Administration
Business Service Center
7th & D Streets, SW
Washington, DC 20407
AREAS SERVICED
*District of Columbia, nearby
Maryland and Virginia

*Consists of District of Columbia, the counties of
Montgomery and Prince George's in Maryland, and the City
of Alexandria and the counties of Arlington, Fairfax, Loudon
and Prince William of Virginia.

Appendix 8

State Aid
for Small Business

S tate programs have become the prime source for
financial assistance. *States tend to be less risk
conscious than traditional institutions and, as
contrasted with banks, don't mind lending small amounts of
money.* Most states (and many counties and cities) have a
program. If you don't see one for your locale listed here,
contact your local chamber of commerce to see if one has
recently been initiated.

Don't forget to check on other programs that may be useful;
for instance, you might sell to or contract with your state.
States are also becoming aggressive on exporting.

Alabama

- For general information, contact:
  (800) 248-0033, (205) 263-0048
  Alabama Development Office
  State Capitol
  Montgomery, AL 36130

- Small Business Innovative Research:
  Alabama has an established SBIR Program and a complementary
  program in the Alabama Innovation Fund.
  Contact: Jim Hatzenbuehler
  (205) 535-2051

Alaska

- For general information, contact:
  (907) 465-2017
  Division of Economic Development
  Department of Commerce and Economic Development
  P.O. Box D
  Juneau, AK 99811

- Small Business Innovative Research:
  Alaska Science and Technology Foundation
  Contact: John W. Siebert
  (907) 272-4333

Arizona

- For general information, contact:
  (602) 280-1341
  Office of Business Finance
  Department of Commerce
  3800 North Central Avenue
  Suite 1500
  Phoenix, AZ 85012

- Small Business Innovative Research:
  Arizona Department of Commerce
  Contact: Donald E. Cline
  (602) 280-1300

Arkansas

- For general information, contact:
  (501) 682-5275
  Small Business Information Center
  Industrial Development Commission
  State Capitol Mall
  Room 4C-300
  Little Rock, AR 72201

- Small Business Innovation Research:
  Arkansas Science and Technology Authority

Contact: Chuck Meyers
(501) 324-9006

- Publications:
  Export Buyers Directory
  International Trade Bulletin
  Starting a Small Business in Arkansas
  Arkansas Industrial Development Commission
  One State Capitol Mall
  Little Rock, AR 72201
  (501) 682-5275

California

- For general information, contact:
  (916) 327-4357; (916) 445-6543
  Office of Small Business
  Department of Commerce
  801 K Street
  Suite 1700
  Sacramento, CA 95814

- Small Business Innovative Research:
  California Department of Commerce
  Contact: Kim Neri
  (916) 324-9538

- Publications:
  Barriers to Agricultural Trade
  California Export Finance Program
  California Export Statistics Study
  California Manufactured Exports
  California Service Exports
  California Trade with Canada and the U.S.
  California World Trade Commission
  Emerging Global Responsibilities Pacific Rim Trade
  International Trade Exhibition Services
  California Department of Commerce
  Office of Small Business
  801 K Street
  Suite 1700
  Sacramento, CA 95814
  (916) 445-6543

Colorado

- For general information, contact:
  (800) 333-7798 ; (303) 592-5920

One-Stop Assistance Center
1560 Broadway
Suite 1530
Denver, CO 80202

- Small Business Innovative Research:
    Colorado Department of Economic Development
    Contact: Rick M. Garcia
    (303) 892-3809

- Publications:
    Colorado Directory of Manufacturers
    Colorado Export Resource Directory
    Colorado International Trade Directory
    Doing Business in Colorado Business Start-up Kits
        Colorado Office of Economic Development
        Small Business Office
        1625 Broadway, Suite 1710
        Denver, CO 80202
        (800) 323-7798 (in state)
        (303) 592-5920 (Denver metropolitan area)
        (303) 892-3840 (all others)

Connecticut

- For general information, contact:
    (203) 258-4269
    Small Business Services
    Department of Economic Development
    865 Brook Street
    Rocky Hill, CT 06067

- Small Business Innovative Research:
    Bridge Grant: Phase I winners are eligible
    for a $20,000 award. Eligibility is lost to
    unsuccessful Phase II applicants.
    Contact: Eric Ott
    (203) 258-4305

- Publications:
    Connecticut Women & Minorities in Business
    Connecticut USA
    Establishing a business in Connecticut
    Licensing Joint Venture and Other Business Opportunities
        Connecticut Department of Economic
         Development
        Small Business Services
        210 Washington Street

Hartford, CT 06106
(203) 566-4051

Delaware

- For general information, contact:
  (302) 739-4271
  Development Office
  P.O. Box 1401
  99 Kings Highway
  Dover, DE 19903

- Small Business Innovative Research:
  Matching Grant: Program will match the amount
  of a Phase I award.
  Contact: Gary Smith
  (302) 739-4271

- Publications:
  Delaware International Guide to Resources
  Exporter Directory
  Small Business Start-up Guides
  Delaware Development Office
  P.O. Box 1401
  99 Kings Highway
  Dover, DE 19903
  (302) 736-4271

District of Columbia

- For general information, contact:
  (202) 727-6600
  Office of Business and Economic Development
  Tenth Floor
  717 14th Street, NW
  Washington, DC 20005

- Publications:
  Export Guide
  International Resource Guide
  Small Business Annual Report
  District of Columbia Office of Business
  and Economic Development
  1111 E Street, NW, Ste. 700
  Washington, DC 20004
  (202) 727-6600

Florida

- For general information, contact:
  (800) 342-0771; (904) 488-9357
  Bureau of Business Assistance
  Department of Commerce
  107 West Gaines Street
  Room 443
  Tallahassee, FL 32399-2000

- Small Business Innovative Research:
  Assistance provided in the preparation of Phase I proposals.
  Contact: Ray Iannucci
  (904) 487-3134

- Publications:
  New Business Guide and Checklist
  Florida Department of Commerce
  Bureau of Business Assistance
  107 W. Gaines Street
  Tallahassee, FL 32339-2000
  (800) 342-0771 (in state)
  (904) 488-9357

Georgia

- For general information, contact:
  (404) 656-6200
  Department of Community Affairs
  100 Peachtree Street
  Suite 1200
  Atlanta, GA 30303

- Small Business Innovative Research:
  Georgia Institute of Technology
  Contact: Vivian Chandler
  (404) 894-3575

- Publications:
  Georgia Manufacturer's Directory
  How to Start a Business in Georgia
  International Trade Directory
  Targeting a Small Business for Export Assistance
  Training Modules on Export Assistance
  Georgia Department of Industry and Trade
  230 Peachtree Street, NW
  Atlanta, GA 30303
  (404) 656-6207

Hawaii

- For general information, contact:
  (808) 548-7645 (808) 543-6691
  Small Business Information Service
  737 Bishop Street
  Suite 1900
  Honolulu, HI 96813

- Small Business Innovative Research:
  Bridge Grants: Phase I winners are eligible for a grant up to 50% of the Phase I award NTE $25,000 subject to availability of funds.
  Contact: Bill Bass
  (808) 625-5293

- Publications:
  Exporters/Importers
  Hawaii Business Abroad
  Hawaii Business Regulation
  Starting a Business in Hawaii
  Hawaii Department of Business
  and Economic Development
  P.O. Box 2359
  Honolulu, HI 96804
  (808) 548-3048

Idaho

- For general information, contact:
  (208) 334-2470
  Economic Development Division
  Department of Commerce
  700 State Street
  Boise, ID 83720-2700

- Small Business Innovative Research:
  Idaho Department of Commerce
  Contact: Karl Tueller
  (208) 334-2470

- Publications:
  Exporter's Guide
  Foreign Language Directory
  How to Start a Small Business in Idaho
  International Trade Directory
  Idaho Department of Commerce
  Economic Development Division
  Department of Commerce

700 State Street
Boise, ID 83720-2700
(208) 334-2470

Illinois

- For general information, contact:
  (800) 252-2923
  Small Business Assistance Bureau
  Department of Commerce and Community Affairs
  620 East Adams Street
  Springfield, IL 62701

- Small Business Innovative Research:
  Bridge Grant: A Phase I awardee between a
  Phase I and Phase II award is eligible to apply
  for a grant equal to its Phase I award.
  Proposal Preparation Assistance: Up to $4,000
  of assistance may be available from a technology
  center to prepare a Phase I proposal.
  Investment Program: Up to $500,000 of assistance
  may be available from the Technology Venture Investment
  Program (TVIP).
  Contact: Lowell Foreman
              (312) 814-2478

- Publications:
  Starting a Small Business in Illinois
  There's No Business Like Small Business in Illinois
              Illinois Department of Commerce and Community Affairs
              Small Business Assistance Bureau
              620 East Adams Street
              Springfield, IL 62701
              (217) 524-5856
  Exporter's Directory
  Illinois Business Services Directory
              Illinois Department of Commerce and Community
              Affairs, International Division
              State of Illinois Center, Ste. 3-400
              100 West Randolph Street
              Chicago, IL 60601
              (312) 917-7164

Indiana

- For general information, contact:
  (800) 824-2476; (317) 232-7304

Ombudsman's Office
Business Development Division
Department of Commerce
One North Capitol
Suite 700
Indianapolis, IN 46204-2288

- Small Business Innovative Research:
  Bridge Funding: Phase I awardees eligible for
  bridge funding up to $50,000.
  Contact: Bill Glennon
  (317) 635-3058

- Publications:
  Guide to Starting a Business in Indiana
  Indiana Directory of International Trade Services
  Indiana Department of Commerce
  One North Capitol
  Suite 700
  Indianapolis, IN 46204-2288
  (317) 232-3527 (Division of Business Expansion)
  (317) 232-8846 (International Trade Division)

Iowa

- For general information, contact:
  (800) 532-1216; (515) 242-4899
  Bureau of Small Business Development
  Department of Economic Development
  200 East Grand Avenue
  Des Moines, IA 50309

- Small Business Innovative Research:
  Proposal Preparation Grant: Phase I program
  may reimburse up to 50% of proposal preparation cost.
  Interim Funding Grant: A Phase I awardee in between
  a Phase I and Phase II award is eligible for up to
  $25,000 in the form of a bridge research grant.
  Contact: Doug Getter
  (515) 242-4704

- Publications:
  Agricultural Machinery Directory for Exporters
  Exporter's Directory
  Food Products for Export
  Iowa World Trade Guide
  Marketing Iowa to the World
  Iowa Department of Economic Development
  New Business Development Division

200 E. Grand Avenue
Des Moines, IA 50309
(800) 532-1216 (in state)
(515) 281-8310 (all others)
(515) 281-7258 (Bureau of International Marketing)

Kansas

- For general information, contact:
  (913) 296-5298
  Division of Existing Industry Development
  400 SW Eighth Street
  Topeka, KS 66603

- Small Business Innovative Research:
  Matching Grant: Program will match the cost
  incurred in proposal development for Phase I and Phase II.
  Contact: Kevin Carr
                    (913) 296-5272

- Publications:
  Directory of Export Manufacturers
  Guide to Starting a Business in Kansas
  International Trade Resource Directory
                    Kansas Department of Commerce
                    Division of Existing Industry Development
                    and Trade Development
                    400 SW Eighth Street, 5th Floor
                    Topeka, KS 66603
                    (913) 296-5298 or (913) 296-4027

Kentucky

- For general information, contact:
  (800) 626-2250; (502) 564-4252
  Division of Small Business
  Capitol Plaza Tower
  Frankfort, KY 40601

- Small Business Innovative Research:
  Bridge Grant: Phase I awardees are eligible
  for 60% of award NTE $30,000. An additional
  $5,000 is available upon receipt of another
  award during the same Federal fiscal year.
  Contact: Ebbie Kimbrough
                    (502) 564-7670

- Publications:
    The Entrepreneur's Guide
        Kentucky Commerce Cabinet
        Small Business Division
        Capitol Plaza Tower, 22nd Floor
        Frankfort, KY 40601
        (800) 626-2250 (in state)
        (502) 564-4252
    Exporter's Directory
    International Trade Directory
        Kentucky Commerce Cabinet
        International Marketing Division
        Capitol Plaza Tower, 24th Floor
        Frankfort, KY 40601
        (502) 564-2170

Louisiana

- For general information, contact:
    (504) 342-5365
    Development Division
    Office of Commerce and Industry
    P.O. Box 94185
    Baton Rouge, LA 70804-9185

- Small Business Innovative Research:
    Matching Fund: A Phase I awardee is eligible
    for matching funds up to $50,000.
    Contact: Mike Williams
        (504) 342-5675

- Publications:
    Economic Advantages of Doing Business in Louisiana
    Guide to International Business for Louisiana
        Companies
    How to Export
    Small Business Financing in Louisiana
        Louisiana Office of Commerce and Industry,
        Finance and Development
        P.O. Box 94185
        Baton Rouge, LA 70804-9185
        (504) 342-5388 (Small Business Consortium)
        (504) 342-9232 (International Trade)

Maine

- For general information, contact:
  (800) 872-3838; (207) 289-3153
  Business Development Division
  State Development Office
  State House
  Augusta, ME 04333

- Small Business Innovative Research:
  Grant Product Development: Program participants
  may be eligible for up to $5,000 for proposal
  assistance and product development.
  Contact: Terry Shehata
  (207) 289-3703

- Publications:
  Doing Business in Maine
  Maine Office of Business Development
  State House Station #59
  Augusta, ME 04333
  (800) 872-3838 (in state)
  (207) 289-2656
  International Commerce Training Guide
  Maine World Trade Association
  77 Sewall Street
  Augusta, ME 04330
  (207) 622-0234

Maryland

- For general information, contact:
  (800) 873-7232; (301) 333-6996
  Division of Business Development
  Department of Economic and Employment Development
  217 East Redwood Street
  Baltimore, MD 21202

- Small Business Innovative Research:
  Maryland Development of Economic and
  Employment Development
  Contact: Selig Solomon
  (301) 333-6990

- Publications:
  Guide to Business Regulation

Suggestions for Developing a Business Plan
>Maryland Office of Business and Industrial Development
>45 Calvert Street
>Annapolis, MD 21401
>(800) 654-7336 (in state)
>(301) 974-2946

Exporter's Guide
Maryland Directory of Exporters
Maryland Resource Directory for International Trade
Trade Fair Assistance Program
>Maryland Office of International Trade
>World Trade Center, 7th Floor
>401 East Pratt Street
>Baltimore, MD 21202
>(301) 333-4295

Massachusetts

- For general information, contact:
  >(617) 727-3206
  >Office of Business Development
  >100 Cambridge Street
  >13th Street
  >Boston, MA 02202

- Publications:
  >***All the Basic Facts You Need to Start a Small Business***
  >***Directory of Biotech Companies***
  >***Directory of Foreign Firms***
  >***Directory of Software Companies***
  >***Export Services Directory***
  >***Software Export Guide***
  >>Massachusetts Department of Commerce
  >>100 Cambridge Street
  >>Boston, MA 02202
  >>Small Business Assistance Division,
  >>13th Floor
  >>(617) 727-4005
  >>Office of International Trade and Investment
  >>Suite 902
  >>(617) 367-1830

Michigan

- For general information, contact:
  >(800) 232-2727; (517) 373-6241
  >Michigan Business Ombudsman

Department of Commerce
P.O. Box 30107
Lansing, MI 48909

- Small Business Innovative Research:
  Michigan Department of Commerce
  Contact: Fred Grasman
  (517) 335-2150

- Publications:
  A Guide to Starting a Business in Michigan
  Michigan Department of Commerce, Business
  Ombudsman
  P.O. Box 30107
  Lansing, MI 48909
  (800) 232-2727 (in state)
  (517) 373-6241
  Michigan Export Directory
  Michigan International Business Services Directory
  Michigan Export Development Authority
  P.O. Box 30017
  4th Floor, N. Ottawa Building
  Lansing, MI 48909
  (517) 373-1054

Minnesota

- For general information, contact:
  (800) 652-9747; (612) 296-3871
  Small Business Assistance Office
  Department of Trade and Economic Development
  900 American Center Building
  150 East Kellogg Blvd.
  St. Paul, MN 55101

- Small Business Innovative Research:
  Minnesota Project Innovation
  Contact: Jim Swiderski
  (612) 338-3280

- Publications:
  A Guide to Starting a Business in Minnesota
  Minnesota Department of Trade and
  Economic Development
  Small Business Assistance Office
  900 American Center Building
  150 E. Kellogg Blvd.
  St. Paul, MN 55101
  (800) 652-9747 (in-state)

(612) 296-3871
Industry Directory
International Business Services Directory
Minnesota Exporter's Assistance Guide
Minnesota Trade Office
1000 World Trade Center
30 E. 7th Street
St. Paul, MN 55101
(612) 297-4222

Mississippi

- For general information, contact:
  (601) 359-3552
  Small Business Bureau
  Research and Development Center
  P.O. Box 849
  Jackson, MS 39205

- Small Business Innovative Research:
  Mississippi Department of Economic
  and Community Development
  Contact: David De Blanc
  (601) 688-3144

- Publications:
  How to Prepare a Business Plan
  Mississippi Manufacturer's Directory
  Mississippi Small Business Development Center
  3825 Ridgewood Rd.
  Jackson, MS 39211-6453
  (601) 982-6231
  Exporter's Handbook
  International Trade Directory
  Mississippi Facts Book
  Department of Economic Development
  Marketing Division
  P.O. Box 849
  Jackson, MS 39205
  (601) 359-3444

Missouri

- For general information, contact:
  (314) 751-4982   (314) 751-8411
  Small Business Development Office
  Department of Economic Development

P.O. Box 118
Jefferson City, MO 65102

- Small Business Innovative Research:
Missouri Department of Economic
Development
Contact: Lisa Kane
(314) 751-3906

- Publications:
Existing Business Resource Directory
International Trade Directory
A Missouri Export Directory
Starting a New Business in Missouri
You Can Export
Missouri Department of Economic Development
P.O. Box 118
Jefferson City, MO 65102
(314) 751-4982 (Small Business Office)
(314) 751-4855 (International Business Division)

Montana

- For general information, contact:
(800) 221-8015, (406) 444-2801
Business Assistance Division
Department of Commerce
1424 Ninth Avenue
Helena, MT 59620

- Small Business Innovative Research:
Montana Department of Commerce
Contact: Elinor W. Edmunds
(406) 449-2778

- Publications:
A Guide to Montana's Economic Development
and Business Assistance Programs
Montana Industrial Relocation Growth
Montana Department of Commerce,
Business Assistance Division
1424 Ninth Avenue
Helena, MT 59620
(800) 221-8015 (in-state)
(406) 444-3923

Nebraska

- For general information, contact:
  (402) 471-3782
  Existing Business Division
  Department of Economic Development
  P.O. Box 94666
  301 Centennial Mall South
  Lincoln, NE 68509-4666

- Small Business Innovative Research:
  Nebraska Research and Development
  Authority (NRDA)
  Contact: Dr. Jack Bishop
           (402) 475-5109

- Publications:
  Export Guide Manual
  International Commerce Guide
  International Trade Directory
  Resource Manual for Nebraska Business
  Ten Steps to Exporting
        Nebraska Department of Economic Development
        P.O. Box 94666
        301 Centennial Mall South
        Lincoln, NE 68509
        (402) 471-4167 (Small Business Division)
        (402) 471-4668 (International Trade)

Nevada

- For general information, contact:
  (702) 687-4325
  Nevada Commission on Economic Development
  Capitol Complex
  Carson City, NV 89710

- Small Business Innovative Research:
  Nevada Commission on Economic
  Development
  Contact: Ray Horner
           (702) 687-4325

- Publications:
  Starting a Small Business in Northern Nevada
        Nevada Office of Community Services
        1100 E. William Street, Ste. 116
        Carson City, NV 89710
        (702) 885-4602 or (702) 855-5978

Agriculture Directory
Export Community in Nevada
Export Directory
> Nevada Commission on Economic Development
> Capitol Complex
> Carson City, NV 89710
> (702) 885-4325

New Hampshire

- For general information, contact:
  (603) 625-4522
  Small Business Development Center
  University Center
  Room 311
  400 Commercial Street
  Manchester, NH 03101

- Publications:
  Business Planning Guide
  Starting a Business in New Hampshire
  > New Hampshire Office of Industrial Development
  > 105 Loudon Road
  > Prescott Park, Building 2
  > Manchester, NH 03101
  > (603) 271-2591

  The Consultant
  Horizons
  So You Want to Export?
  > New Hampshire Small Business Development Center
  > International Trade Association
  > 400 Commercial Street, Room 311
  > Manchester, NH 03101
  > (603) 625-4522

New Jersey

- For general information, contact:
  (609) 984-4442
  Office of Small Business Assistance
  Department of Commerce and
  Economic Development
  20 West State Street, CN835
  Trenton, NJ 08625

- Small Business Innovative Research:

SBIR applications may receive:

- Advice in preparing new proposals
or revising resubmissions

- Technical assistance and faculty
participation from state sponsored
advanced technology centers
Contact: Joe Montemarano
(609) 984-1671

- Publications:
Start-up Kits
New Jersey Department of Commerce and
Economic Development
Office of Small Business Assistance
20 West State Street, CN 835
Trenton, NJ 08625
(609) 984-4442
International Report (Monthly)
New Jersey Guide to Export Assistance
New Jersey International Trade News
New Jersey Department of Commerce,
Energy & Economic Development
Division of International Trade
100 Mulberry Street, Gateway 4, 10th Floor
Newark, NJ 07102
(201) 648-3518

New Mexico

- For general information, contact:
(505) 827-0300
Economic Development Division
Department of Economic Development
1100 St. Francis Drive
Santa Fe, NM 87503

- Small Business Innovative Research:
Economic Development Department
of New Mexico
Contact: Ponzi Ferraccio
(505) 827-0300

- Publications:
International Trade Directory
Preparing a Business Plan
New Mexico Economic Development and
Tourism Department

1100 St. Francis Dr.
Santa Fe, NM 87503
(505) 827-0315

New York

- For general information, contact:
  (212) 827-6150
  Division for Small Business
  Department of Economic Development
  1515 Broadway
  51st Floor
  New York, NY 10036
- Small Business Innovative Research:

  - **Technical assistance** in the use of
    SBIR Program research undertaken,
    and commercialization.

  - **Bridge funding** of up to $50,000 per active Phase II proposers;
    eligibility and selection criteria apply.
    Contact: Owen Goldfarb
                    (518) 473-9746

- Publications:
  Export Opportunities Bulletin
  Selling to Foreign Markets
  Your Business: A Management Guide for Small Business
          New York Department of Economic Development
          1515 Broadway, 51st Floor
          New York, NY 10036
          (212) 827-6150 (Division of Small Business)
          (212) 827-6208 (Division of International Commerce)

North Carolina

- For general information, contact:
  (919) 733-7980
  Small Business Development
  Department of Economic and
  Community Development
  Dobbs Building
  Room 2019
  430 North Salisbury Street
  Raleigh, NC 27611

- Small Business Innovative Research:
  Technology Development Authority of North Carolina
  Contact: Brent Lane
  (919) 733-7022

- Publications:
  Big Answers to Small Business Questions
  Guidelines on Starting a Business, Registering
  a Business Name and Organizing a Business
  Corporation in North Carolina
  International Report
  North Carolina Department of Commerce
  430 N. Salisbury Street
  Raleigh, NC 27611
  (919) 733-7980 (Small Business Development Division)
  (919) 733-7193 (International Division)

North Dakota

- For general information, contact:
  (701) 224-2810
  Small Business Coordinator
  Economic Development Commission
  Liberty Memorial Building
  604 East Blvd.
  Bismarck, ND 58505

- Small Business Innovative Research:
  Technical Assistance and Funding
  Contact: Bruce Gjovig
  (701) 777-3132

- Publications:
  Exporters Guide
  Manufacturer's Guide
  North Dakota Guide to International Trade
  Steps to Starting a Business
  North Dakota Economic Development Commission
  Liberty Memorial Building
  Bismark, ND 58505
  (800) 472-2100 (in state)
  (701) 224-2810

Ohio

- For general information, contact:
  (800) 248-4040; (614) 466-4232

Small and Developing Business Division
Department of Development
P.O. Box 1001
Columbus, Ohio 43266-0101

- Small Business Innovative Research:

  - **Technical Assistance Centers**:
  Network of seven centers statewide
  to provide assistance in proposals
  preparation

  - **Bridge Grants**: Phase I awardees are eligible for a $35,000
  award NTE amount of Phase I award. Eligibility lost for
  unsuccessful Phase II proposers.
  Contact: G. Mark Skinner
  (614) 466-5867

- Publications:
    Export Report
    Export Service Directory
    International Business Opportunities
          Ohio Department of Development
          International Trade Division
          P.O. Box 1001
          Columbus, OH 43266
          (800) 282-1085 (in state)
          (614) 466-5017

Oklahoma

- For general information, contact:
    (800) 477-6552; (405) 843-9770
    Oklahoma Department of Commerce
    P.O. Box 26980
    6601 N. Broadway Extension
    Oklahoma City, OK 73126-0980

- Small Business Innovative Research:

  - **Phase I Incentive Funding**: Phase I proposers are eligible for
  50% of proposal preparation cost on a reimbursement basis
  NTE $3,000.

  - **Matching Fund**: Phase I awardees are eligible for a state
  matching award equal to 50% of Phase I amount NTE $25,000
  upon submission of a Federal Phase II proposal.
  Contact: Sherilyn Stickley
  (405) 848-2633

- Publications:
  OSBDC Newsletter
  > Oklahoma Department of Commerce
  > 6601 Broadway Extension
  > Oklahoma City, OK 73116-8214
  > (405) 843-9770
  > (405) 521-2401 (International Trade Division)

Oregon

- For general information, contact:
  > (800) 233-3306; (503) 373-1200
  > Economic Development Department
  > 775 Summer Street NE
  > Salem, OR 97310

- Publications:
  Services for Oregon Businesses
  > Oregon Economic Development Department
  > Small Business Division
  > 595 Cottage Street, NE
  > Salem, OR 97310
  > (800) 233-3306 (in-state)
  > (503) 373-1200

  Directory of Oregon Manufacturers
  Oregon Exporter's Handbook
  Oregon International Trade Directory
  > Oregon Economic Development
  > International Trade Division
  > One World Trade Center, Ste. 300
  > 121 SW Salmon
  > Portland, OR 97204
  > (503) 229-5625

Pennsylvania

- For general information, contact:
  > (717) 783-5700
  > Bureau of Small Business and Appalachian Development
  > Department of Commerce
  > 461 Forum Building
  > Harrisburg, PA 17120

- Small Business Innovative Research:
  > Technology Assistance Centers
  > Pennsylvania Department of Commerce

        Contact: William J. Cook
                    (717) 787-4147

- Publications:
    Export Opportunities Bulletin
    Resource Directory for Small Business
    Starting a Small Business in Pennsylvania
            Pennsylvania Department of Commerce
            Forum Building
            Harrisburg, PA 17120
            Business Resource Network, Rm. 404
            (717) 783-5700
            Bureau for International Development, Rm. 489
            (717) 787-7190

Puerto Rico

- For general information, contact:
    (809) 721-3290
    Commonwealth Department of Commerce
    Box S
    4275 Old San Juan Station
    San Juan, PR 00905

- Publications:
    Products and Services in Puerto Rico
            Puerto Rico Department of Commerce
            Program of Foreign Trade
            P.O. Box S-4275
            San Juan, PR 00905
            (809) 721-3290

Rhode Island

- For general information, contact:
    (401) 277-2601
    Business Development Division
    Department of Economic Development
    Seven Jackson Walkway
    Providence, RI 02903

- Small Business Innovative Research:

    - Phase I proposers are eligible for a $1,000 award NTE 3 such
      awards in one year.

    - A Phase I awardee that uses a university faculty member as a
      consultant in the planning or research phase of its Phase I

  proposal is eligible to receive 50% of the consultant's fee NTE
  $2,500.

- A Phase I awardee that has submitted a Phase II proposal is
  eligible to receive 50% of the Phase I award NTE $25,000.
  This award becomes a no interest bridge loan if a Phase II
  award is made.
  Contact: Claudia Terra
      (401) 277-2601

- Publications:
  Deadline
  Export
  Guide to International Trade in Rhode Island
  Starting a Business in Rhode Island
    Department of Economic Development
    7 Jackson Walkway
    Providence, RI 02903
    (401) 277-2601

South Carolina

- For general information, contact:
  (800) 922-6684; (803) 737-0888
  Enterprise Development
  P.O. Box 1149
  Columbia, SC 29202

- Small Business Innovative Research:
  Alternative Assistance Program
  Contact: John Lenti
      (803) 777-5118

- Publications:
  Business Formation & Expansion Manual
  Export Resource Directory
    South Carolina State Department Board
    Business Development and Assistance Division
    P.O. Box 927
    Columbia, SC 29202
    (803) 737-0400

South Dakota

- For general information, contact:
  (800) 872-6190 (605) 773-5032
  Governor's Office of Economic Development
  Capital Lake Plaza

711 Wells Avenue
Pierre, SD 57501

- Small Business Innovative Research:
  Alternative Assistance Program
  Contact: Melvin Ustad
                    (605) 256-5555

- Publications:
  Business Start-Up Kits
  Export Directory
          Governor's Office of Economic Development
          Capitol Lake Plaza
          Pierre, SD 57501
          (800) 952-3625 (in state)
          (605) 773-5032

Tennessee

- For general information, contact:
  (800) 872-7201; (615) 741-2626
  Small Business Office
  Department of Economic and Community Development
  320 Sixth Avenue North
  Seventh Floor
  Rachel Jackson Building
  Nashville, TN 37219

- Small Business Innovative Research:
  The Tennessee Technology Foundation offers technical assistance
  in proposal preparation, evaluation, and recommendations and
  provides matching services with capital venture sources.
  Contact: Dr. David A. Patterson
                    (615) 694-6772

- Publications:
  A Guide to Doing Business in Tennessee
  Guide to Exporters' Services
  International Trade Directory
          Department of Economic and Community Development
          Rachel Jackson Building, 7th Floor
          320 6th Avenue, N.
          Nashville, TN 37219
          (800) 872-7201 (in-state)
          (615) 741-2626 (Small Business Office)
          (615) 741-5870 (Office of Export Trade Promotion)

Texas

- For general information, contact:
    (800) 888-0511; (512) 472-5059
    Small Business Division
    Department of Commerce
    Economic Development Commission
    P.O. Box 12728
    Capitol Station
    410 East Fifth Street
    Austin, TX 78711

- Small Business Innovative Research:
    Product Development and Commercialization Funds
    Contact: Annette Argall
                (512) 320-9407

- Publications:
    The Business Plan: A Suggested Model
    International Trade Partners
    Results
    Texas Small Business Minority Directory
                Texas Department of Commerce
                P.O. Box 12728
                410 E. 5th Street
                Austin, TX 78711
                (512) 472-5059

Utah

- For general information, contact:
    (801) 581-7905
    Small Business Development Center
    102 West 500 South
    Suite 315
    Salt Lake City, UT 84101

- Small Business Innovative Research:
    Utah Technology Finance Corporation
    Contact: Robert Brewer
                (801) 581-6348

- Publications:
    Business Planning Guide
    Going into Business in Utah: Playing the Game
                Utah Small Business Development Center
                660 S. 200 East, Ste. 418
                Salt Lake City, UT 84111
                (801) 581-7905

Utah Export Directory
Department of Economic Development,
International Division
State Office Building, #6150
Salt Lake City, UT 84114
(801) 538-3052

Vermont

* For general information, contact:
  (800) 622-4553 (802) 828-3221
  Agency of Development and Community Affairs
  The Pavilion
  109 State Street
  Montpelier, VT 05609

* Publications:
  Doing Business in Vermont
  Vermont Buyer's Guide
  Vermont Economic Development Department
  109 State Street
  Montpelier, VT 05602
  (802) 828-3221

Virginia

* For general information, contact:
  (804) 371-8252
  Small Business and Financial Services
  Department of Economic Development
  P.O. Box 798
  1000 Washington Building
  Richmond, VA 23206

* Small Business Innovative Research: Provides direct
  commercialization assistance to Phase II awardees. Also available
  is research matching assistance for SBIR proposers.
  Contact: Dave Miller
  (703) 689-3025

* Publications:
  Establishing a Business in Virginia
  Virginia Business Resource Directory
  Virginia Department of Economic Development,
  Small Business & Financial Services
  1000 Washington Building, 9th Floor
  Richmond, VA 23219
  (805) 786-3791

Directory of Virginia's Exporters and Importers
International Business Services Directory
Department of World Trade
6000 World Trade Center
Norfolk, VA 23510
(804) 683-2849

Washington

- For general information, contact:
  (509) 335-1576
  Small Business Development Center
  245 Todd Hall
  Washington State University
  Pullman, WA 99164-4727

- Small Business Innovative Research:
  State of Washington Department of Trade
  Contact: Barbara A Campbell
  (206) 586-0265

- Publications:
  Operating a Home-based Business in Washington
  Starting a Business in Washington
  Washington State University
  441 Todd Hall
  Pullman, WA 99164
  (509) 335-1576
  Exporter's Guide
  Face to Face
  Washington State Trader
  Department of Trade
  312 First Avenue, North
  Seattle, WA 98109
  (206) 464-7076

West Virginia

- For general information, contact:
  (304) 348-2960
  Small Business Development Center Division
  1115 Virginia Street, East
  Charleston, WV 25301

- Small Business Innovative Research:
  Governor's Office of Community and Industrial Development
  Contact: Lori Walker
  (304) 348-2234

- <u>Publications:</u>
  International Buyers Guide
  Starting a Business in West Virginia
  West Virginia International Report
  > Governor's Office of Community and Industrial Development
  > State Capitol Complex
  > Charleston, WV 25305
  > (304) 348-2960 (Small Business Development
  >   Center Division)
  > (304) 348-0400 (International Development Division)

Wisconsin

- For general information, contact:
  (800) 435-7287 (609) 266-1018
  Public Information Bureau
  Department of Development
  P.O. Box 7970
  123 West Washington Avenue
  Madison, WI 53707

- Small Business Innovative Research:

  - **Advisory Proposal Review for Phase I Proposals**: Phase I
    applicants may request to have their Phase I proposals critiqued
    prior to submission by a 2-person team consisting of (1) a
    university scientist and (2) a representative from a successful
    SBIR company.

  - **Bridge Financing**: Phase I awardees are eligible for a loan up
    to $40,000 while in between a Phase I and Phase II award (25%
    of the loan amount must be matched by the award recipient). If
    the research project does not lead to product
    commercialization, then the loan is treated as a grant.
    Contact: Caroline Garber
    > (608) 267-9383

- <u>Publications:</u>
  Wisconsin Business Start-up Kits
  Wisconsin International Trade
  > Wisconsin Department of Development
  > P.O. Box 7970
  > 123 West Washington Avenue
  > Madison, Wisconsin 53707
  > (608) 266-0562 or (608) 266-1480

Wyoming

- For general information, contact:
  (307) 777-7287
  Economic Development and Stabilization Board
  Herschler Building
  Cheyenne, Wyoming 82002

- Small Business Innovative Research:
  State of Wyoming - Department of Commerce -
  Division of Economic Community Development.
  Contact: Paul Howard
  (307) 777-6433

- Publications:
  Wyoming International trade Directory
  International Trade Office
  Herschler Bldg., 3rd Floor, East
  Cheyenne, WY 82002
  (307) 777-6412

Appendix 9

Quick Reference Federal Contacts

Agricultural Marketing Service, USDA	(202) 447-8998
Animal Care, APHIS/USDA	(301) 436-7799
Antitrust Division, USDOJ	(202) 633-3543
Aquaculture Information Center	(301) 344-3704
Bureau of Indian Affairs, DOI	(202) 343-4576
Capitol, U.S.	(202) 225-6827
Census Bureau, USDOC	(301) 763-4100
Commodity Futures Trading Commission	(202) 254-8630
Congressional Record, GPO, Subscriptions	(202) 783-3238
Congressional Record Index, unpublished	(202) 275-9009
Congressional Research Service	(202) 707-5700
Consumer Product Safety Commission	(800) 638-2772
Cooperative Extension Service, USDA	(202) 447-3029
Copyrights Information, Library of Congress	(202) 479-0700
Application Forms Request	(202) 707-9100
Customs Service, Treasury Department	(800) 872-3253
Economic Development Administration, USDOC	(202) 377-4085
Education, DOE, Financial Aid Information	
Bilingual Clearinghouse	(800) 336-4560
Energy Inquiry and Referral	(800) 523-2929
Appropriate Technology Assistance	(800) 428-2525
EPA Chemical Emergency Preparedness	(800) 535-0202
RCRA Superfund Hotline	(800) 424-9346
Pesticides Telecommunications Network	(800) 858-7378

Small Business Hotline	(800) 368-5888
Radon/Asbestos Hotline	(800) 334-8571
Export/Import Bank	(800) 424-5201
Farm Credit Administration	(703) 883-4251
Farmers Home Administration, USDA	(202) 475-4100
Federal Communications Commission,	
Common Carrier/Mass Media Bureau,	
Small Business Assistance	(202) 632-7000
Federal Crime Insurance	(800) 638-8780
Federal Deposit Insurance Corp.	(800) 424-5488
Federal Election Commission	(800) 424-9530
Federal Emergency Management Agency	(800) 838-8820
Federal Home Loan Bank Board	(800) 424-5404
Federal Information Center, GSA	(800) 347-1997
Federal Highway Administration, USDOT	(202) 366-4853
Federal Register (Nat'l Archives), GPO	(202) 783-3238
Statutes Unit	(202) 523-6641
Public Laws Update Service (PLUS)	(202) 523-6641
Flood Insurance Program, FEMA	(800) 638-6620
Food & Nutrition Service, USDA	(703) 756-3276
Forest Service, USDA	(404) 347-4177
Garment Registration Number, FTC	(202) 326-3034
General Accounting Office, Documents	(202) 275-6241
General Services Administration,	
Small Business Service Centers	(404) 331-5103
Government Printing Office, Publications	(202) 783-3238
Housing & Urban Development, USHUD	(202) 755-6950
Immigration & Naturalization Service, USDOJ	(800) 777-7700
Internal Revenue Service, Treasury Department	(800) 829-1040
	(800) 829-3676
Labor/Management Standards, USDOL	(202) 523-7343
Labor Surplus Areas, USDOL	(202) 535-0189
Library of Congress	(202) 707-5000
Meat & Poultry Inspection, FSIS/USDA	(800) 535-4555
Metric Conversion Program, USDOC	(202) 377-0944
National Archives	(202) 501-5000
National Credit Union Administration	(202) 682-9600
National Institutes of Health,	
Office of Technology Transfer	(301) 496-0750
National Labor Relations Board	(202) 254-9430
National Marine Fishery Service,	
USDOC/NOAA/NMFS	
Seafood Inspection Service	(301) 427-2355
National Technical Information Service, USDOC	(800) 336-4700

Oil & Chemical Spills, Natl. Response Center,	
USCG/USDOT	(800) 424-8802
Overseas Private Investment Corp.	(800) 424-6742
Passport Services, USDOS	(202) 647-2424
Patent & Trademark Office, USDOC,	(703) 557-3341
Pension Planning, IRS, SEPs #590	(202) 566-6783
Pension/Welfare Benefits Admin., USDOL	(202) 523-8921
Southeastern Regional Educational Improvement	
Laboratory, USDOE,	(919) 549-8216
Resolution Trust Corporation,	
Contractor Registration Office	(800) 541-1782
Rural Information Center,	
National Agricultural Library	
& the Cooperative Extension Service,	(301) 344-5414
Security & Exchange Commission - Filings	(202) 272-7450
SBA Answer Desk,	(800) 827-5722
	(800) 827-5722
Smithsonian Institute	(202) 357-2700
Social Security Administration	(800) 772-1213
U.S. Postal Service	(202) 268-2000
Veterans Affairs	(202) 376-6996
Visa Services, USDOS	(202) 647-0510
White House, 1600 Pennsylvania Avenue,	(202) 456-7041
Women's Economic Development Corps.	(800) 222-2933
Weather Service, USDOC	(301) 427-7258
Weights & Measures, National Institute of Standards	
& Technology (NIST) USDOC,	(301) 975-4004

HOTLINES: The NIST maintains these hotlines with recorded messages which give weekly updates for international businesses.

GATT HOTLINE	(301) 975-4041
EC-92 HOTLINE	(301) 921-4164

Index

X

Y

U

V

W

The Business Bookshelf

These books have been carefully selected as the best on these subjects. **Your satisfaction is guaranteed or your money back.**

To order, call toll-free (800) 255-5730 extension 110. Please have your Visa, Mastercard, American Express or Discover card ready.

Money Sources for Small Business
How You Can Find Private, State, Federal, and Corporate Financing

By William Alarid. Many potential successful business owners simply don't have enough cash to get started. *Money Sources* shows how to get money from Federal, State, Venture Capital Clubs, Corporations, Computerized Matching Services, Small Business Investment Companies plus many other sources. Includes samples of loan applications.

ISBN 0-940673-51-7 224 pages 8½x11 paperbound $19.95
See special offer on last page!

Small Time Operator
How to Start Your Own Business, Keep Your Books, Pay Your Taxes, and Stay Out of Trouble

By Bernard Kamaroff, C.P.A. The most popular small business book in the U.S., it's used by over 250,000 businesses. Easy to read and use, *Small Time Operator* is particularly good for those without book-keeping experience. Comes complete with a year's supply of ledgers and worksheets designed especially for small businesses, and contains invaluable information on permits, licenses, financing, loans, insurance, bank accounts, etc.

ISBN 0-917510-06-2 190 pages 8½x11 paperbound $12.95

**Puma Publishing • 1670 Coral Drive, Suite 3E
Santa Maria, California 93454**

The Business Planning Guide
Creating a Plan for Success in Your Own Business
By Andy Bangs. *The Business Planning Guide* has been used by hundreds of banks, colleges, and accounting firms to guide business owners through the process of putting together a complete and effective business plan and financing proposal. The *Guide* comes complete with examples, forms and worksheets that make the planning process painless. With over 150,000 copies in print, the *Guide* has become a small business classic.
ISBN 0-936894--10-5 149 pages 8½x11 paperbound $18.95

Free Help from Uncle Sam to Start Your Own Business
(Or Expand the One You Have) 3rd Edition
By William Alarid and Gustav Berle. *Free Help* describes over 100 government programs that help small business and give dozens of examples of how others have used this aid. Included are appendices with helpful books, organizations and phone numbers.
ISBN 0-940673-54-1 304 pages 5½x8½ paperbound $13.95

Marketing Without Advertising
By Michael Phillips and Salli Rasberry. A creative and practical guide that shows small business people how to avoid wasting money on advertising. The authors, experienced business consultants, show how to implement an ongoing marketing plan to tell potential and current customers that yours is a quality business worth trusting, recommending, and coming back to.
ISBN 0-87337-019-8 200 pages 8½x11 paperbound $13.95

The Partnership Book
By attorneys Dennis Clifford and Ralph Warner. When two or more people join to start a small business, one of the most basic needs is to establish a solid, legal partnership agreement. This book supplies a number of sample agreements which you can use as is. Buy-out clauses, unequal sharing of assets, and limited partnerships are all discussed in detail.
ISBN 0-87337-141-0 221 pages 8½x11 paperbound $24.95

Call Toll-Free (800) 255-5730 extension 110.
Please have Visa, Mastercard, American Express or Discover card ready, or write: Puma Publishing, 1670 Coral Drive, Suite 3E, Santa Maria, California 93454.
Sales Tax: Please add 7¾% for shipping to California addresses.
Shipping $2.00 per book; airmail $4.00 per book.

More Millions of Dollars
May Be Sitting Unused

(Now at a discount price)

Find *more* millions of dollars for small business that *are sitting unused.* Since you've purchased *Free Help From Uncle Sam* we're offering a special discount on:

Money Sources for Small Business:
How You Can Find
Private, State, Federal and Corporate Financing
(See description on previous page)

$14.95 postpaid, airmail
(regularly $19.95 plus tax and $4.00 airmail)

To get this discount, cut out or copy this page and mail to:

PUMA PUBLISHING
1670 CORAL DRIVE • SANTA MARIA, CA 93454
This discount available by mail only.

Firm Name: _____

Your Name: _____

Address: _____

City:_____ State:_____ Zip:_____

Payment: ☐ Check   ☐ Credit Card _____

No. _____ Expires_____

To help us get to know our customers better, please supply the following information (optional):

Occupation:_____

Age (check one):   ☐ Over 40   ☐ Under 40